CL

ONE HUNDR

CLASSIC *f*M
ONE HUNDRED
FAVOURITE
POEMS

Introduction and biographies of the poets by
Mike Read

Hodder & Stoughton

Compilation © Classic FM 1997
Poems © Individual copyright holders

Foreword, introduction and biographies of the poets
© Mike Read 1997, 2000

First published by Hodder & Stoughton in 1997
A division of Hodder Headline

This revised edition published
by Hodder & Stoughton in 2001

26 27

Typeset by Hewer Text Ltd, Edinburgh
Printed and bound by Mackays of Chatham PLC

ISBN 0 340 71320 8

Hodder & Stoughton
A division of Hodder Headline
338 Euston Road
London
NW1 3BH

CLASSIC *f*M

ONE HUNDRED FAVOURITE POEMS

Contents

vii

Classic FM Top One Hundred Poems

Foreword to the new edition

Little did we imagine when we decided to publish a book of the Classic FM listeners' favourite poems that it would be so successful. Now, three years and 50,000 copies later, we have taken this opportunity to reset the text to match the larger, easier-to-read type of the equally successful *Classic FM Humorous Poems*. We have also been able to include some of the longer poems in full for the first time, though entries like *Paradise Lost* and *Hiawatha* are so long that it would be impractical in those cases.

It's interesting to speculate whether the Top 100 would be different if we repeated the poll now. I suspect not, but I'm sure the wonderful work of the organisers of National Poetry Day will result in more people enjoying contemporary poetry and not just the classics.

In the meanwhile, I hope you enjoy this selection, whether you're reading it yourself or listening to all those great actors performing the poems on the audiobook!

Mike Read
October 2000

Introduction

I've always loved to read and write poetry, so when I was asked by Classic FM to contribute to the series *My Favourite Room* I asked if I could deliver the piece in the form of a poem. After its broadcast I rather surprisingly received dozens of letters asking for a copy, which led me to realise that there were a lot of listeners who also enjoyed poetry.

Before the previous statement is mistaken for vanity, I should point out that my enthusiasm was tempered with the realisation that if some forty people out of 5 million appreciated it, maybe the remaining 4,999,960 might well have received it with a bored equanimity. However, one poem led to another and the idea of reading one every morning was born. This is the poem that started it all.

A ROOM WITH BOOKS

There's a feeling in a room with books, the love
The depth the warmth of something that's alive.
The ranks and rows of old campaigners stand
Passed from hand to hand, friend to friend, to me.
The flames in shadow dance upon them all,
Who themselves once danced upon this earth;

Burns, Belloc, Blunden, Bridges, Beardsley, Brooke;
Inscribed with care from lover; mother; friend
Hughes, Hardy, Henley, Hopkins, Hugo, Hood;
In faded hand 'December 1910'.
Books from the libraries of Laureates,
Volumes revered as Bibles at the Front,
Classics, passions, open wounds, injustice.
As full-bodied wine, verse, chapter, stanza;
Spill and flow out across the floodlit lawns,
From leathered desk to some dark, secret place.
And here I sit, surrounded by my friends,
Their words remain though they themselves are gone,
Their lives re-lived within my favourite room.

As well as the poems voted into the Top 100 by Classic
FM listeners, I thought it would make the anthology a little
different if I wrote a potted history of each of the poets. The
earliest poet in the Top 100 is Christopher Marlowe, born
just two months before Shakespeare and eight years before
John Donne, while the only poet in the list not to reach his
twentieth birthday is John Gillespie Magee. Entrants Walter
de la Mare and Wilfrid Gibson were both heirs to the estate
of fellow Top 100 poet Rupert Brooke, while the only one-
legged writers to appear on the list are W. H. Davies and W.
E. Henley. Rugby appears to be the best-represented
school, with St Paul's in second place. The Top 100 features
two Lords and two Knights, including Sir John Betjeman
who, at six entries, has more titles on the list than any other
poet.

Each poem's position in the Top 100 appears above its

title and we have arranged the poems in alphabetical order of the poets' names. This gives an interesting mixture of poems from different ages and enables the reader to see all of a chosen poet's work together.

Acknowledgements are due to Lindsay Dear, Tim Lihoreau and Will Sussman at Classic FM for all their help in assembling the Classic FM Poetry Top 100, and to BREAKFAST MILK™ for their generous sponsorship of the broadcasts.

Mike Read

MATTHEW ARNOLD
1822–88

———— ⊶⊷ ————

Born at Laleham-on-Thames, Middlesex, on Christmas Eve 1822, he was the son of the redoubtable Dr Thomas Arnold, headmaster of Rugby School from 1828 to 1842. The younger Arnold was educated at Rugby and Winchester before going up to Balliol College, Oxford, where he became a close friend of fellow poet Arthur Hugh Clough. Both men became Fellows of Oriel College. In 1851 Arnold became an Inspector of Schools, a job which took him the length and breadth of the country for the next thirty-five years. In 1851 he married Fanny Lucy Wightman; the couple had six children, but had to cope with the loss of three sons in infancy.

Arnold had won the Newdigate Prize at Oxford for a poem on Cromwell, and his poetic output continued unabated throughout his life; in later years, however, he began to turn to prose. As a respected critic in the literary, social and educational fields, he believed strongly that England should be more European in its outlook: no doubt today he would have been a passionate supporter of greater European integration. He began his poem 'Dover Beach' on his honeymoon, while 'The Scholar Gypsy' was published in 1853.

Arnold died in Liverpool on 15 April 1888, whilst waiting to meet his newly married daughter on her return from America.

Matthew Arnold

DOVER BEACH

The sea is calm to-night.
The tide is full, the moon lies fair
Upon the Straits; – on the French coast, the light
Gleams, and is gone; the cliffs of England stand,
Glimmering and vast, out in the tranquil bay.
Come to the window, sweet is the night air!
Only, from the long line of spray
Where the ebb meets the moon-blanch'd sand,
Listen! you hear the grating roar
Of pebbles which the waves suck back, and fling,
At their return, up the high strand,
Begin, and cease, and then again begin,
With tremulous cadence slow, and bring
The eternal note of sadness in.

  Sophocles long ago
Heard it on the Aegean, and it brought
Into his mind the turbid ebb and flow
Of human misery; we
Find also in the sound a thought,
Hearing it by this distant northern sea.

The sea of faith
Was once, too, at the full, and round earth's shore
Lay like the folds of a bright girdle furl'd;

But now I only hear
Its melancholy, long, withdrawing roar,
Retreating to the breath
Of the night-wind down the vast edges drear
And naked shingles of the world.

Ah, love, let us be true
To one another! for the world, which seems
To lie before us like a land of dreams,
So various, so beautiful, so new,
Hath really neither joy, nor love, nor light,
Nor certitude, nor peace, nor help for pain;
And we are here as on a darkling plain
Swept with confused alarms of struggle and flight,
Where ignorant armies clash by night.

76

THE SCHOLAR GIPSY

Go, for they call you, Shepherd, from the hill;
  Go, Shepherd, and untie the wattled cotes:
    No longer leave thy wistful flock unfed,
  Nor let thy bawling fellows rack their throats,
    Nor the cropp'd herbage shoot another head.
      But when the fields are still,
  And the tired men and dogs all gone to rest,
    And only the white sheep are sometimes seen
    Cross and recross the strips of moon-blanch'd green;
Come, Shepherd, and again renew the quest.

Here, where the reaper was at work of late,
  In this high field's dark corner, where he leaves
    His coat, his basket, and his earthen cruise,
  And in the sun all morning binds the sheaves,
    Then here, at noon, comes back his stores to use;
      Here will I sit and wait,
  While to my ear from uplands far away
    The bleating of the folded flocks is borne;
    With distant cries of reapers in the corn –
All the live murmur of a summer's day.

Screen'd is this nook o'er the high, half-reap'd field,
  And here till sun-down, Shepherd, will I be.

Through the thick corn the scarlet poppies peep
And round green roots and yellowing stalks I see
   Pale pink convolvulus in tendrils creep:
     And air-swept lindens yield
Their scent, and rustle down their perfum'd showers
   Of bloom on the bent grass where I am laid,
   And bower me from the August sun with shade;
And the eye travels down to Oxford's towers:

And near me on the grass lies Glanvil's book –
   Come, let me read the oft-read tale again,
    The story of that Oxford scholar poor,
Of pregnant parts and quick inventive brain,
    Who, tir'd of knocking at Preferment's door,
     One summer morn forsook
His friends, and went to learn the Gipsy lore,
   And roam'd the world with that wild brotherhood,
   And came, as most men deem'd, to little good,
But came to Oxford and his friends no more.

But once, years after, in the country lanes,
   Two scholars, whom at college erst he knew,
    Met him, and of his way of life enquir'd.
Whereat he answer'd, that the Gipsy crew,
    His mates, had arts to rule as they desir'd
     The workings of men's brains;
And they can bind them to what thoughts they will:
   'And I,' he said, 'the secret of their art,
   When fully learn'd, will to the world impart:
But it needs happy moments for this skill.'

This said, he left them, and return'd no more. –
   But rumours hung about the country side,
     That the lost Scholar long was seen to stray,
   Seen by rare glimpses, pensive and tongue-tied,
     In hat of antique shape, and cloak of grey,
       The same the Gipsies wore.
   Shepherds had met him on the Hurst in spring:
     At some lone alehouse in the Berkshire moors,
     On the warm ingle bench, the smock-frock'd boors
   Had found him seated at their entering,

But, 'mid their drink and clatter, he would fly:
   And I myself seem half to know thy looks,
     And put the shepherds, Wanderer, on thy trace;
   And boys who in lone wheatfields scare the rooks
     I ask if thou hast pass'd their quiet place;
       Or in my boat I lie
   Moor'd to the cool bank in the summer heats,
     Mid wide grass meadows which the sunshine fills,
     And watch the warm, green-muffled Cumner hills,
   And wonder if thou haunt'st their shy retreats.

For most, I know, thou lov'st retired ground.
   Thee, at the ferry, Oxford riders blithe,
     Returning home on summer nights, have met
   Crossing the stripling Thames at Bab-lock-hithe,
     Trailing in the cool stream thy fingers wet,
       As the slow punt swings round:

And leaning backward in a pensive dream,
    And fostering in thy lap a heap of flowers
    Pluck'd in shy fields and distant Wychwood bowers,
And thine eyes resting on the moonlit stream.

And then they land, and thou art seen no more.
    Maidens, who from the distant hamlets come
    To dance around the Fyfield elm in May,
Oft through the darkening fields have seen thee roam,
    Or cross a stile into the public way.
      Oft thou hast given them store
Of flowers – the frail-leaf'd, white anemone –
    Dark bluebells drench'd with dews of summer eves –
    And purple orchises with spotted leaves –
But none has words she can report of thee.

And, above Godstow Bridge, when hay-time's here
    In June, and many a scythe in sunshine flames,
    Men who through those wide fields of breezy grass
Where black-wing'd swallows haunt the glittering
    Thames,
    To bathe in the abandon'd lasher pass,
      Have often pass'd thee near
Sitting upon the river bank o'ergrown:
    Mark'd thine outlandish garb, thy figure spare,
    Thy dark vague eyes, and soft abstracted air;
But, when they came from bathing, thou wert gone.

Matthew Arnold

At some lone homestead in the Cumner hills,
   Where at her open door the housewife darns,
      Thou hast been seen, or hanging on a gate
   To watch the threshers in the mossy barns.
      Children, who early range these slopes and late
        For cresses from the rills,
   Have known thee watching, all an April day,
      The springing pastures and the feeding kine;
      And mark'd thee, when the stars come out and shine,
   Through the long dewy grass move slow away.

In autumn, on the skirts of Bagley Wood,
   Where most the Gipsies by the turf-edg'd way
      Pitch their smok'd tents, and every bush you see
   With scarlet patches tagg'd and shreds of grey,
      Above the forest ground called Thessaly –
        The blackbird picking food
   Sees thee, nor stops his meal, nor fears at all;
      So often has he known thee past him stray,
      Rapt, twirling in thy hand a wither'd spray,
   And waiting for the spark from Heaven to fall.

And once, in winter, on the causeway chill
   Where home through flooded fields foot-travellers go,
      Have I not pass'd thee on the wooden bridge
   Wrapt in thy cloak and battling with the snow,
      Thy face towards Hinksey and its wintry ridge?

And thou hast climb'd the hill,
And gain'd the white brow of the Cumner range,
    Turn'd once to watch, while thick the snow-flakes fall,
    The line of festal light in Christ-Church hall –
Then sought thy straw in some sequester'd grange.

But what – I dream! Two hundred years are flown
    Since first thy story ran through Oxford halls,
        And the grave Glanvil did the tale inscribe
    That thou wert wander'd from the studious walls
        To learn strange arts, and join a Gipsy tribe:
            And thou from earth art gone
    Long since, and in some quiet churchyard laid;
        Some country nook, where o'er thy unknown grave
        Tall grasses and white flowering nettles wave –
Under a dark red-fruited yew-tree's shade.

– No, no, thou hast not felt the lapse of hours.
    For what wears out the life of mortal men?
        'Tis that from change to change their being rolls:
    'Tis that repeated shocks, again, again,
        Exhaust the energy of strongest souls,
            And numb the elastic powers.
    Till having us'd our nerves with bliss and teen,
        And tired upon a thousand schemes our wit,
        To the just-pausing Genius we remit
Our worn-out life, and are – what we have been.

Thou hast not lived, why should'st thou perish, so?
  Thou hadst *one* aim, *one* business, *one* desire:
    Else wert thou long since number'd with the dead –
  Else hadst thou spent, like other men, thy fire.
    The generations of thy peers are fled,
      And we ourselves shall go;
  But thou possessest an immortal lot,
    And we imagine thee exempt from age
    And living as thou liv'st on Glanvil's page,
  Because thou hadst – what we, alas, have not!

For early didst thou leave the world, with powers
  Fresh, undiverted to the world without,
    Firm to their mark, not spent on other things;
  Free from the sick fatigue, the languid doubt,
    Which much to have tried, in much been baffled,
    brings.
      O Life unlike to ours!
  Who fluctuate idly without term or scope,
    Of whom each strives, nor knows for what he strives,
    And each half lives a hundred different lives;
  Who wait like thee, but not, like thee, in hope.

Thou waitest for the spark from Heaven: and we,
  Light half-believers of our casual creeds,
    Who never deeply felt, nor clearly will'd,
  Whose insight never has borne fruit in deeds,
    Whose vague resolves never have been fulfill'd:

For whom each year we see
Breeds new beginnings, disappointments new;
   Who hesitate and falter life away,
   And lose to-morrow the ground won to-day –
Ah! do not we, Wanderer! await it too?

Yes, we await it, but it still delays,
   And then we suffer; and amongst us One,
     Who most has suffer'd, takes dejectedly
His seat upon the intellectual throne;
     And all his store of sad experience he
       Lays bare of wretched days;
Tells us his misery's birth and growth and signs,
   And how the dying spark of hope was fed,
   And how the breast was sooth'd, and how the head,
And all his hourly varied anodynes.

This for our wisest: and we others pine,
   And wish the long unhappy dream would end,
     And waive all claim to bliss, and try to bear
With close-lipp'd Patience for our only friend,
     Sad Patience, too near neighbour to Despair:
       But none has hope like thine.
Thou through the fields and through the woods dost
   stray,
   Roaming the country side, a truant boy,
   Nursing thy project in unclouded joy,
And every doubt long blown by time away.

Matthew Arnold

O born in days when wits were fresh and clear,
   And life ran gaily as the sparkling Thames;
      Before this strange disease of modern life,
   With its sick hurry, its divided aims,
      Its heads o'ertax'd, its palsied hearts, was rife –
         Fly hence, our contact fear!
   Still fly, plunge deeper in the bowering wood!
      Averse, as Dido did with gesture stern
      From her false friend's approach in Hades turn,
   Wave us away, and keep thy solitude!

Still nursing the unconquerable hope,
   Still clutching the inviolable shade,
      With a free, onward impulse brushing through,
   By night, the silver'd branches of the glade –
      Far on the forest skirts, where none pursue,
         On some mild pastoral slope
   Emerge, and resting on the moonlit pales,
      Freshen thy flowers, as in former years,
      With dew, or listen with enchanted ears,
   From the dark dingles, to the nightingales.

But fly our paths, our feverish contact fly!
   For strong the infection of our mental strife,
      Which, though it gives no bliss, yet spoils for
         rest;
   And we should win thee from thy own fair life,
      Like us distracted, and like us unblest.

Soon, soon thy cheer would die,
Thy hopes grow timorous, and unfix'd thy powers.
And thy clear aims be cross and shifting made:
And then thy glad perennial youth would fade,
Fade, and grow old at last and die like ours.

Then fly our greetings, fly our speech and smiles!
– As some grave Tyrian trader, from the sea,
Descried at sunrise an emerging prow
Lifting the cool-hair'd creepers stealthily,
The fringes of a southward-facing brow
Among the Ægæan isles;
And saw the merry Grecian coaster come,
Freighted with amber grapes, and Chian wine,
Green bursting figs, and tunnies steep'd in brine;
And knew the intruders on his ancient home,

The young light-hearted Masters of the waves;
And snatch'd his rudder, and shook out more sail;
And day and night held on indignantly
O'er the blue Midland waters with the gale,
Betwixt the Syrtes and soft Sicily,
To where the Atlantic raves
Outside the Western Straits; and unbent sails
There, where down cloudy cliffs, through sheets of
foam,
Shy traffickers, the dark Iberians come;
And on the beach undid his corded bales.

W. H. AUDEN
1907–73

Wystan Hugh Auden was born on 21 February 1907 in York, the third son of Dr G. A. Auden, who was inspired by memories of his schooldays when it came to choosing a name for the boy. Dr Auden had been a pupil at Repton in Derbyshire, and the nearby parish church is dedicated to St Wystan. At the age of eight, young Wystan was sent to St Edmund's School, Hindhead, Surrey; here he met Christopher Isherwood, who was to become a lifelong personal and literary friend.

Auden was already a published poet by the time he went up to Christ Church, Oxford, where his friends included John Betjeman, Cecil Day-Lewis, Louis MacNeice and Stephen Spender. Among his tutors was J. R. R. Tolkien, who inspired Auden with something of his own passion for Anglo-Saxon and Middle English poetry. During the 1930s Auden established himself as both a poet and a playwright, working at times in collaboration with Isherwood and with the composer Benjamin Britten, whom he met while attached to the GPO Film Unit. His move to America on the eve of war in 1939 was heavily criticised, and it took him some time to regain his former popularity. Nevertheless he was appointed Professor of Poetry at Oxford in 1956 and made a Fellow of Christ Church in 1962. He died at his house in Kirchstetten, Austria, on 29 September 1973.

'Stop All the Clocks' became phenomenally popular after its inclusion in the 1994 film *Four Weddings and a Funeral*, while 'Night Mail' was written, as its name suggests, during Auden's time with the GPO Film Unit.

W. H. Auden

38

STOP ALL THE CLOCKS
from TWELVE SONGS

Stop all the clocks, cut off the telephone,
Prevent the dog from barking with a juicy bone,
Silence the pianos and with muffled drum
Bring out the coffin, let the mourners come.

Let aeroplanes circle moaning overhead
Scribbling on the sky the message He Is Dead,
Put crepe bows round the white necks of the public doves,
Let the traffic policemen wear black cotton gloves.

He was my North, my South, my East and West,
My working week and my Sunday rest,
My noon, my midnight, my talk, my song;
I thought that love would last for ever: I was wrong.

The stars are not wanted now: put out every one;
Pack up the moon and dismantle the sun;
Pour away the ocean and sweep up the wood.
For nothing now can ever come to any good.

W. H. Auden

39

NIGHT MAIL

I

This is the Night Mail crossing the Border,
Bringing the cheque and the postal order,

Letters for the rich, letters for the poor,
The shop at the corner, the girl next door.

Pulling up Beattock, a steady climb:
The gradient's against her, but she's on time.

Past cotton-grass and moorland boulder,
Shovelling white steam over her shoulder,

Snorting noisily, she passes
Silent miles of wind-bent grasses.

Birds turn their heads as she approaches,
Stare from bushes at her blank-faced coaches.

Sheep-dogs cannot turn her course;
They slumber on with paws across.

In the farm she passes no one wakes,
But a jug in a bedroom gently shakes.

II

Dawn freshens. Her climb is done.
Down towards Glasgow she descends,
Towards the steam tugs yelping down a glade of cranes,
Towards the fields of apparatus, the furnaces
Set on the dark plain like gigantic chessmen.
All Scotland waits for her:
In dark glens, beside pale-green lochs,
Men long for news.

III

Letters of thanks, letters from banks,
Letters of joy from girl and boy,
Receipted bills and invitations
To inspect new stock or to visit relations,
And applications for situations,
And timid lovers' declarations,
And gossip, gossip from all the nations,
News circumstantial, news financial,
Letters with holiday snaps to enlarge in,
Letters with faces scrawled on the margin,
Letters from uncles, cousins and aunts,
Letters to Scotland from the South of France,
Letters of condolence to Highlands and Lowlands,
Written on paper of every hue,
The pink, the violet, the white and the blue,
The chatty, the catty, the boring, the adoring,
The cold and official and the heart's outpouring,
Clever, stupid, short and long,
The typed and the printed and the spelt all wrong.

IV

Thousands are still asleep,
Dreaming of terrifying monsters
Or a friendly tea beside the band in Cranston's or
    Crawford's:
Asleep in working Glasgow, asleep in well-set
    Edinburgh,
Asleep in granite Aberdeen,
They continue their dreams,
But shall wake soon and hope for letters,
And none will hear the postman's knock
Without a quickening of the heart.
For who can bear to feel himself forgotten?

HILAIRE BELLOC
1870–1953

Belloc was born near Paris of a French father and an English mother. The Franco-Prussian War of 1870–1 resulted in the destruction of the Belloc family property, and the future writer and his parents fled to London.

After his mother's death in 1891 Belloc led a semi-nomadic existence, lecturing across America and publishing books on touring France by bicycle. Sussex has already laid claim to being his spiritual home, and it was to Slindon in West Sussex that Belloc, his wife Elodie and their growing family moved in 1905. Despite his opponent's slogan 'Don't Vote for a Frenchman and a Catholic!' Belloc took Salford for the Liberals at the 1906 election and was to remain an MP for some years. He later left the Liberals and teamed up with his great friend G. K. Chesterton to form what Shaw dubbed the one entity 'Chesterbelloc' in their many ideological disputes.

A prolific author, Belloc published 153 books during his lifetime. He is probably best remembered for his 'Cautionary Tales'.

In 1906 he bought 'Kingsland' at Shipley in Sussex, complete with a working mill and five acres of land, for one thousand pounds, where he lived until his death.

84

TARANTELLA

Do you remember an Inn,
Miranda?
Do you remember an Inn?
And the tedding and the spreading
Of the straw for a bedding,
And the fleas that tease in the High Pyrenees,
And the wine that tasted of the tar,
And the cheers and the jeers of the young muleteers
(Under the vine of the dark verandah)?
Do you remember an Inn, Miranda?
Do you remember an Inn?
And the cheers and the jeers of the young muleteers
Who hadn't got a penny,
And who weren't paying any,
And the hammer at the doors and the Din?
And the Hip! Hop! Hap!
Of the clap
Of the hands to the twirl and the swirl
Of the girl gone chancing,
Glancing,
Dancing,
Backing and advancing,
Snapping of the clapper to the spin
Out and in –
And the Ting, Tong, Tang of the Guitar!

Do you remember an Inn,
Miranda?
Do you remember an Inn?
Never more;
Miranda,
Never more.
Only the high peaks' hoar:
And Aragon a torrent at the door.
No sound
In the walls of the Halls where falls
The tread
Of the feet of the dead to the ground
No sound:
But the boom
Of the far Waterfall like Doom.

SIR JOHN BETJEMAN
1906–84

━━━━⚬⚬⚬━━━━

John Betjemann (note the extra 'n') was born on 28 August 1906 in London and was first educated at the local Highgate Junior School, where his teachers included T. S. Eliot. He then moved via the Dragon School in Oxford to Marlborough, where he met Louis MacNeice and the subsequent art historian and spy Anthony Blunt. Family holidays were spent each summer on the North Cornish coast, where he began his lifelong passion for Cornwall. Schoolboy taunts at his Germanic-sounding name during the First World War led to the dropping of the extra 'n', and it was as Betjeman that he went up to Magdalen College, Oxford, where his circle included Osbert Lancaster, W. H. Auden and Lionel Perry. He detested his tutor, C. S. Lewis, and much preferred the charismatic don Maurice Bowra.

After leaving Oxford without a degree, Betjeman was briefly a schoolmaster, then worked for Shell as Editor of their Town Guides and for the *Architectural Review*. An increasingly popular poet and early television personality, he founded the Victorian Society in 1958 and published his long autobiographical poem *Summoned by Bells* in 1960, the same year that he was awarded the CBE. Further honours followed: he was knighted in 1968, and appointed Poet Laureate in 1974. After a long battle with Parkinson's disease he died on 19 May 1984 in his beloved Cornwall, where he now lies buried in the churchyard at St Endoc. He is perhaps the most popular poet in the Classic FM Poetry Top 100, with no fewer than six poems included.

26

CHRISTMAS

The bells of waiting Advent ring,
  The Tortoise stove is lit again
And lamp-oil light across the night
  Has caught the streaks of winter rain
In many a stained-glass window sheen
From Crimson Lake to Hooker's Green.

The holly in the windy hedge
  And round the Manor House the yew
Will soon be stripped to deck the ledge,
  The altar, font and arch and pew,
So that the villagers can say
'The church looks nice' on Christmas Day.

Provincial public houses blaze
  And Corporation tramcars clang,
On lighted tenements I gaze
  Where paper decorations hang,
And bunting in the red Town Hall
Says 'Merry Christmas to you all.'

And London shops on Christmas Eve
  Are strung with silver bells and flowers
As hurrying clerks the City leave
  To pigeon-haunted classic towers,

And marbled clouds go scudding by
The many-steepled London sky.

And girls in slacks remember Dad,
   And oafish louts remember Mum,
And sleepless children's hearts are glad,
   And Christmas-morning bells say 'Come!'
Even to shining ones who dwell
Safe in the Dorchester Hotel.

And is it true? And is it true,
   This most tremendous tale of all,
Seen in a stained-glass window's hue,
   A Baby in an ox's stall?
The Maker of the stars and sea
Become a Child on earth for me?

And is it true? For if it is,
   No loving fingers tying strings
Around those tissued fripperies,
   The sweet and silly Christmas things,
Bath salts and inexpensive scent
And hideous tie so kindly meant,

No love that in a family dwells,
   No carolling in frosty air,
Nor all the steeple-shaking bells,
   Can with this single Truth compare –
That God was Man in Palestine
And lives to-day in Bread and Wine.

33

DIARY OF A CHURCH MOUSE

Here among long-discarded cassocks,
Damp stools, and half-split open hassocks,
Here where the Vicar never looks
I nibble through old service books.
Lean and alone I spend my days
Behind this Church of England baize.
I share my dark forgotten room
With two oil-lamps and half a broom.
The cleaner never bothers me,
So here I eat my frugal tea.
My bread is sawdust mixed with straw;
My jam is polish for the floor.
　Christmas and Easter may be feasts
For congregations and for priests,
And so may Whitsun. All the same,
They do not fill my meagre frame.
For me the only feast at all
Is Autumn's Harvest Festival,
When I can satisfy my want
With ears of corn around the font.
I climb the eagle's brazen head
To burrow through a loaf of bread.
I scramble up the pulpit stair
And gnaw the marrows hanging there.
　It is enjoyable to taste

These items ere they go to waste,
But how annoying when one finds
That other mice with pagan minds
Come into church my food to share
Who have no proper business there.
Two field mice who have no desire
To be baptized, invade the choir.
A large and most unfriendly rat
Comes in to see what we are at.
He says he thinks there is no God
And yet he comes . . . it's rather odd.
This year he stole a sheaf of wheat
(It screened our special preacher's seat),
And prosperous mice from fields away
Come in to hear the organ play,
And under cover of its notes
Ate through the altar's sheaf of oats.
A Low Church mouse, who thinks that I
Am too papistical, and High,
Yet somehow doesn't think it wrong
To munch through Harvest Evensong,
While I, who starve the whole year through,
Must share my food with rodents who
Except at this time of the year
Not once inside the church appear.

Within the human world I know
Such goings-on could not be so,
For human beings only do
What their religion tells them to.
They read the Bible every day

And always, night and morning, pray,
And just like me, the good church mouse,
Worship each week in God's own house,
   But all the same it's strange to me
How very full the church can be
With people I don't see at all
Except at Harvest Festival.

47

A SUBALTERN'S LOVE-SONG

Miss J. Hunter Dunn, Miss J. Hunter Dunn,
Furnish'd and burnish'd by Aldershot sun,
What strenuous singles we played after tea,
We in the tournament – you against me!

Love-thirty, love-forty, oh! weakness of joy,
The speed of a swallow, the grace of a boy,
With carefullest carelessness, gaily you won,
I am weak from your loveliness, Joan Hunter Dunn.

Miss Joan Hunter Dunn, Miss Joan Hunter Dunn,
How mad I am, sad I am, glad that you won.
The warm-handled racket is back in its press,
But my shock-headed victor, she loves me no less.

Her father's euonymus shines as we walk,
And swing past the summer-house, buried in talk,
And cool the verandah that welcomes us in
To the six-o'clock news and a lime-juice and gin.

The scent of the conifers, sound of the bath,
The view from my bedroom of moss-dappled path,
As I struggle with double-end evening tie,
For we dance at the Golf Club, my victor and I.

On the floor of her bedroom lie blazer and shorts
And the cream-coloured walls are be-trophied with sports,
And westering, questioning settles the sun
On your low-leaded window, Miss Joan Hunter Dunn.

The Hillman is waiting, the light's in the hall,
The pictures of Egypt are bright on the wall,
My sweet, I am standing beside the oak stair
And there on the landing's the light on your hair.

By roads 'not adopted', by woodlanded ways,
She drove to the club in the late summer haze,
Into nine-o'clock Camberley, heavy with bells
And mushroomy, pine-woody, evergreen smells.

Miss Joan Hunter Dunn, Miss Joan Hunter Dunn,
I can hear from the car-park the dance has begun.
Oh! full Surrey twilight! importunate band!
Oh! strongly adorable tennis-girl's hand!

Around us are Rovers and Austins afar,
Above us, the intimate roof of the car,
And here on my right is the girl of my choice,
With the tilt of her nose and the chime of her voice,

And the scent of her wrap, and the words never said,
And the ominous, ominous dancing ahead.
We sat in the car-park till twenty to one
And now I'm engaged to Miss Joan Hunter Dunn.

95

HUNTER TRIALS

It's awf'lly bad luck on Diana,
   Her ponies have swallowed their bits;
She fished down their throats with a spanner
   And frightened them all into fits.

So now she's attempting to borrow.
   Do lend her some bits, Mummy, *do*;
I'll lend her my own for to-morrow,
   But to-day *I*'ll be wanting them too.

Just look at Prunella on Guzzle,
   The wizardest pony on earth;
Why doesn't she slacken his muzzle
   And tighten the breech in his girth?

I say, Mummy, there's Mrs Geyser
   And doesn't she look pretty sick?
I bet it's because Mona Lisa
   Was hit on the hock with a brick.

Miss Blewitt says Monica threw it,
   But Monica says it was Joan,
And Joan's very thick with Miss Blewitt,
   So Monica's sulking alone.

And Margaret failed in her paces,
    Her withers got tied in a noose,
So her coronet's caught in the traces
    And now all her fetlocks are loose.

Oh, it's me now. I'm terribly nervous.
    I wonder if Smudges will shy.
She's practically certain to swerve as
    Her Pelham is over one eye.

*

Oh wasn't it naughty of Smudges?
    Oh, Mummy, I'm sick with disgust.
She threw me in front of the Judges,
    And my silly old collarbone's bust.

98

MYFANWY

Kind o'er the *kinderbank* leans my Myfanwy,
  White o'er the play-pen the sheen of her dress,
Fresh from the bathroom and soft in the nursery
  Soap-scented fingers I long to caress.

Were you a prefect and head of your dormit'ry?
  Were you a hockey girl, tennis or gym?
Who was your favourite? Who had a crush on you?
  Which were the baths where they taught you to swim?

Smooth down the Avenue glitters the bicycle,
  Black-stockinged legs under navy-blue serge,
Home and Colonial, Star, International,
  Balancing bicycle leant on the verge.

Trace me your wheel-tracks, you fortunate bicycle,
  Out of the shopping and into the dark,
Back down the Avenue, back to the pottingshed,
  Back to the house on the fringe of the park.

Golden the light on the locks of Myfanwy,
  Golden the light on the book on her knee,
Finger-marked pages of Rackham's Hans Andersen,
  Time for the children to come down to tea.

Sir John Betjeman

Oh! Fuller's angel-cake, Robertson's marmalade,
  Liberty lampshade, come, shine on us all,
My! what a spread for the friends of Myfanwy
  Some in the alcove and some in the hall.

Then what sardines in the half-lighted passages!
  Locking of fingers in long hide-and-seek.
You will protect me, my silken Myfanwy,
  Ringleader, tom-boy, and chum to the weak.

99

SLOUGH

Come, friendly bombs, and fall on Slough
It isn't fit for humans now,
There isn't grass to graze a cow
    Swarm over, Death!

Come, bombs, and blow to smithereens
Those air-conditioned, bright canteens,
Tinned fruit, tinned meat, tinned milk, tinned beans
    Tinned minds, tinned breath.

Mess up the mess they call a town –
A house for ninety-seven down
And once a week a half-a-crown
    For twenty years,

And get that man with double chin
Who'll always cheat and always win,
Who washes his repulsive skin
    In women's tears,

And smash his desk of polished oak
And smash his hands so used to stroke
And stop his boring dirty joke
    And make him yell.

But spare the bald young clerks who add
The profits of the stinking cad;
It's not their fault that they are mad,
    They've tasted Hell.

It's not their fault they do not know
The birdsong from the radio,
It's not their fault they often go
    To Maidenhead

And talk of sports and makes of cars
In various bogus Tudor bars
And daren't look up and see the stars
    But belch instead.

In labour-saving homes, with care
Their wives frizz out peroxide hair
And dry it in synthetic air
    And paint their nails.

Come, friendly bombs, and fall on Slough
To get it ready for the plough.
The cabbages are coming now;
    The earth exhales.

WILLIAM BLAKE
1757–1827

Blake was born on 28 November 1757, the third son of a London hosier. Instead of attending school he was apprenticed to a Covent Garden engraver, and then became a student at the Royal Academy before taking a job as engraver in a bookshop. There he met several of the literary contacts who were to finance the publication of his first poetic work in 1783. In the following year he set up a print shop in Broad Street which enabled him to engrave and publish his own work. Much of his writing was influenced by his deep interest in mysticism, but many considered him to be insane and his work incoherent. His admirers, by contrast, saw in him a visionary whose work was both prophetic and profound. He died on 12 August 1827, hoping to the last that England's 'green and pleasant land' would one day experience the kind of spiritual renaissance which he preached in the preface to his 1804 poem on Milton. This preface, set to music by Sir Hubert Parry in 1915, is of course 'Jerusalem', Blake's best-known work apart from 'The Tyger'.

48

THE TYGER

Tyger! Tyger! burning bright
In the forests of the night,
What immortal hand or eye
Could frame thy fearful symmetry?

In what distant deeps or skies
Burnt the fire of thine eyes?
On what wings dare he aspire?
What the hand dare seize the fire?

And what shoulder, & what art,
Could twist the sinews of thy heart?
And when thy heart began to beat,
What dread hand? & what dread feet?

What the hammer? what the chain?
In what furnace was thy brain?
What the anvil? what dread grasp
Dare its deadly terrors clasp?

When the stars threw down their spears,
And water'd heaven with their tears,
Did he smile his work to see?
Did he who made the Lamb make thee?

William Blake

Tyger! Tyger! burning bright
In the forests of the night,
What immortal hand or eye,
Dare frame thy fearful symmetry?

RUPERT BROOKE
1887–1915

Rupert Brooke was born on 3 August 1887, the son of a Rugby schoolmaster. His interest in poetry was fired by reading Browning, and at Rugby he won poetry prizes as well as playing cricket and rugby. At King's College, Cambridge, he threw himself into university activities, immersing himself in the Drama and the Fabian Society, debating at the Union and becoming a member of the elite group known as the Apostles. It was at this period that he moved to his beloved Grantchester, just outside Cambridge, but an unhappy love affair in addition to other pressures culminated in a nervous breakdown.

The guiding hand of his main literary mentor Edward Marsh and his relationship with the actress Cathleen Nesbitt aided his recovery but he decided to clear his head through travel – to Canada, America and the South Sea Islands. After the outbreak of the First World War he joined the newly formed Royal Naval Division, and saw action in Antwerp before dying of septicaemia on 23 April 1915 en route for Gallipoli. Brooke was buried on the island of Skyros in the Aegean.

Rupert Brooke

8

THE SOLDIER

If I should die, think only this of me:
  That there's some corner of a foreign field
That is for ever England. There shall be
  In that rich earth a richer dust concealed;
A dust whom England bore, shaped, made aware,
  Gave, once, her flowers to love, her ways to roam,
A body of England's, breathing English air,
  Washed by the rivers, blest by suns of home.

And think, this heart, all evil shed away,
  A pulse in the eternal mind, no less
    Gives somewhere back the thoughts by England given;
Her sights and sounds; dreams happy as her day;
  And laughter, learnt of friends; and gentleness,
    In hearts at peace, under an English heaven.

14

From THE OLD VICARAGE, GRANTCHESTER
(Café des Westens, Berlin, May 1912)

Just now the lilac is in bloom,
All before my little room;
And in my flower-beds, I think,
Smile the carnation and the pink;
And down the borders, well I know,
The poppy and the pansy blow . . .
Oh! there the chestnuts, summer through,
Beside the river make for you
A tunnel of green gloom, and sleep
Deeply above; and green and deep
The stream mysterious glides beneath,
Green as a dream and deep as death.
– Oh, damn! I know it! and I know
How the May fields all golden show,
And when the day is young and sweet,
Gild gloriously the bare feet.
That run to bathe . . .
                              Du lieber Gott!

Here am I, sweating, sick, and hot,
And there the shadowed waters fresh
Lean up to embrace the naked flesh.
Temperamentvoll German Jews
Drink beer around; – and *there* the dews

Are soft beneath a morn of gold.
Here tulips bloom as they are told;
Unkempt about those hedges blows
An English unofficial rose;
And there the unregulated sun
Slopes down to rest when day is done,
And wakes a vague unpunctual star,
A slippered Hesper; and there are
Meads towards Haslingfield and Coton
Where *das Betreten*'s not *verboten*.

Ειυε γεψοιμηψ . . . would I were
In Grantchester, in Grantchester! –
Some, it may be, can get in touch
With Nature there, or Earth, or such.
And clever modern men have seen
A Faun a-peeping through the green,
And felt the Classics were not dead,
To glimpse a Naiad's reedy head,
Or hear the Goat-foot piping low: . . .
But these are things I do not know.
I only know that you may lie
Day-long and watch the Cambridge sky,
And, flower-lulled in sleepy grass,
Hear the cool lapse of hours pass.
Until the centuries blend and blur
In Grantchester, in Grantchester . . .
Still in the dawnlit waters cool
His ghostly Lordship swims his pool,
And tries the strokes, essays the tricks,

Long learnt on Hellespont, or Styx.
Dan Chaucer hears his river still
Chatter beneath a phantom mill.
Tennyson notes, with studious eye,
How Cambridge waters hurry by . . .
And in that garden, black and white,
Creep whispers through the grass all night;
And spectral dance, before the dawn,
A hundred Vicars down the lawn;
Curates, long dust, will come and go
On lissom, clerical, printless toe;
And oft between the boughs is seen
The sly shade of a Rural Dean . . .
Till, at a shiver in the skies,
Vanishing with Satanic cries,
The prim ecclesiastic rout
Leaves but a startled sleeper-out,
Grey heavens, the first bird's drowsy calls,
The falling house that never falls.

God! I will pack, and take a train,
And get me to England once again!
For England's the one land, I know,
Where men with Splendid Hearts may go;
And Cambridgeshire, of all England,
The shire for Men who Understand;
And of *that* district I prefer
The lovely hamlet Grantchester.
For Cambridge people rarely smile,
Being urban, squat, and packed with guile . . .

Rupert Brooke

Ah God! to see the branches stir
Across the moon at Grantchester!
To smell the thrilling-sweet and rotten
Unforgettable, unforgotten
River-smell, and hear the breeze
Sobbing in the little trees.
Say, do the elm-clumps greatly stand
Still guardians of that holy land?
The chestnuts shade, in reverend dream,
The yet unacademic stream?
Is dawn a secret shy and cold
Anadyomene, silver-gold?
And sunset still a golden sea
From Haslingfield to Madingley?
And after, ere the night is born,
Do hares come out about the corn?
Oh, is the water sweet and cool,
Gentle and brown, above the pool?
And laughs the immortal river still
Under the mill, under the mill?
Say, is there Beauty yet to find?
And Certainty? and Quiet kind?
Deep meadows yet, for to forget
The lies, and truths, and pain? . . . Oh! yet
Stands the Church clock at ten to three?
And is there honey still for tea?

59

THE GREAT LOVER

I have been so great a lover: filled my days
So proudly with the splendour of Love's praise,
The pain, the calm, and the astonishment,
Desire illimitable, and still content,
And all dear names men use, to cheat despair,
For the perplexed and viewless streams that bear
Our hearts at random down the dark of life.
Now, ere the unthinking silence on that strife
Steals down, I would cheat drowsy Death so far,
My night shall be remembered for a star
That outshone all the suns of all men's days.
Shall I not crown them with immortal praise
Whom I have loved, who have given me, dared with me
High secrets, and in darkness knelt to see
The inenarrable godhead of delight?
Love is a flame: – we have beaconed the world's night,
A city: – and we have built it, these and I.
An emperor: – we have taught the world to die.
So, for their sakes I loved, ere I go hence,
And the high cause of Love's magnificence,
And to keep loyalties young, I'll write those names
Golden for ever, eagles, crying flames,
And set them as a banner, that men may know,
To dare the generations, burn, and blow
Out on the wind of Time, shining and streaming . . .

These I have loved:
      White plates and cups, clean-gleaming,
Ringed with blue lines; and feathery, faery dust;
Wet roofs, beneath the lamp-light; the strong crust.
Of friendly bread; and many-tasting food;
Rainbows; and the blue bitter smoke of wood;
And radiant raindrops couching in cool flowers;
And flowers themselves, that sway through sunny hours,
Dreaming of moths that drink them under the moon;
Then, the cool kindliness of sheets, that soon
Smooth away trouble; and the rough male kiss
Of blankets; grainy wood; live hair that is
Shining and free; blue-massing clouds; the keen
Unpassioned beauty of a great machine;
The benison of hot water; furs to touch;
The good smell of old clothes; and others such –
The comfortable smell of friendly fingers,
Hair's fragrance, and the musty reek that lingers
About dead leaves and last year's ferns . . .
                            Dear names,
And thousand other throng to me! Royal flames;
Sweet water's dimpling laugh from tap or spring;
Holes in the ground; and voices that do sing;
Voices in laughter, too; and body's pain,
Soon turned to peace; and the deep-panting train;
Firm sands; the little dulling edge of foam
That browns and dwindles as the wave goes home;
And washen stones, gay for an hour; the cold
Graveness of iron; moist black earthen mould;
Sleep; and high places; footprints in the dew;

And oaks; and brown horse-chestnuts, glossy-new;
And new-peeled sticks; and shining pools on grass; —
All these have been my loves. And these shall pass.
Whatever passes not, in the great hour,
Nor all my passion, all my prayers, have power
To hold them with me through the gate of Death.
They'll play deserter, turn with the traitor breath,
Break the high bond we made, and sell Love's trust
And sacramented covenant to the dust.
— Oh, never a doubt but, somewhere, I shall wake,
And give what's left of love again, and make
New friends, now strangers . . .
                  But the best I've known
Stays here, and changes, breaks, grows old, is blown
About the winds of the world, and fades from brains
Of living men, and dies.
                Nothing remains
O dear my loves, O faithless, once again
This one last gift I give: that after men
Shall know, and later lovers, far-removed,
Praise you, 'All these were lovely'; say, 'He loved.'

ELIZABETH BARRETT BROWNING
1806–61

———— ⟨⟨⟨⟨ ————

She was born on 6 March 1806, the eldest of the twelve children of Edward Moulton Barrett, whose interests in plantations in Jamaica had made the family wealthy. A childhood riding accident left her with a damaged spine, and a serious illness in 1838 exacerbated her overbearing father's tendency to treat her as an invalid. Although physically weak, she was intellectually strong, with a passion for the classics and a circle of acquaintances which included the leading literary lights of the day.

It was after the Barrett family moved to 50 Wimpole Street, London, an address to become famous in a stage play and two films, that she met Robert Browning and, in the face of her tyrannical father's objection to the relationship, eloped. The couple were married in St Marylebone Parish Church and escaped Mr Barrett's vengeance by moving to Florence, where their only child, Robert, was born in 1849. Her reputation was so high that, on the death of Wordsworth in 1850, she was deemed to be a serious candidate for the vacancy of Poet Laureate. The Brownings travelled extensively and their friends included Tennyson, Thackeray, Carlyle and Ruskin. Elizabeth Barrett Browning died in Florence on 29 June 1861.

18

HOW DO I LOVE THEE?
from Sonnets from the Portuguese

XLIII

How do I love thee? Let me count the ways.
I love thee to the depth and breadth and height
My soul can reach, when feeling out of sight
For the ends of Being and ideal Grace.
I love thee to the level of everyday's
Most quiet need, by sun and candlelight.
I love thee freely, as men strive for Right;
I love thee purely, as they turn from Praise.
I love thee with the passion put to use
In my old griefs, and with my childhood's faith.
I love thee with a love I seemed to lose
With my lost saints, – I love thee with the breath,
Smiles, tears, of all my life! – and, if God choose,
I shall but love thee better after death.

ROBERT BROWNING
1812–89

Browning was born in Camberwell, South London, on 7 May 1812, the son of a clerk in the Bank of England whose extensive library provided his son with many happy hours. Among his early loves were the works of Byron, Keats and Shelley, inspiring him as a twelve-year-old to write a volume of lyric poems.

Following an education mainly at home, he briefly attended London University before abandoning his studies in 1828. Five years later his first poem was published anonymously but failed to cause much of a stir. In 1836 he travelled to Russia, but was unable to secure the diplomatic post he wanted. Nevertheless his poetry was slowly finding an audience.

In September 1846, following a year-long correspondence and courtship, he secretly married Elizabeth Barrett. The couple went to Italy, settling at the Casa Guidi in Florence where, in 1849, their son Robert, known as Pen, was born. After Elizabeth's death in 1861 Browning returned to live in London, subsequently receiving an honorary degree from Oxford University and an honorary fellowship from Balliol College.

He continued to write extensively throughout the 1860s and 1870s, and his enormous popularity led to the founding of the Browning Society in 1881. In addition to his poetry, he also wrote two essays on his fellow poets Shelley and the ill-fated Thomas Chatterton.

Browning died in Venice, on 12 December 1889, and was buried in Westminster Abbey.

4

HOME-THOUGHTS FROM ABROAD

Oh, to be in England
Now that April's there,
And whoever wakes in England
Sees, some morning, unaware,
That the lowest boughs and the brushwood sheaf
Round the elm-tree bole are in tiny leaf,
While the chaffinch sings on the orchard bough
In England – now!

And after April, when May follows,
And the whitethroat builds, and all the swallows –
Hark! where my blossomed pear-tree in the hedge
Leans to the field and scatters on the clover
Blossoms and dewdrops – at the bent spray's edge –
That's the wise thrush; he sings each song twice over,
Lest you should think he never could recapture
The first fine careless rapture!
And though the fields look rough with hoary dew,
All will be gay when noontide wakes anew
The buttercups, the little children's dower,
– Far brighter than this gaudy melon-flower!

75

From THE PIED PIPER

There was a rustling, that seemed like a bustling
Of merry crowds justling at pitching and hustling,
Small feet were pattering, wooden shoes clattering,
Little hands clapping and little tongues chattering,
And, like fowls in a farmyard when barley is scattering,
Out came the children running.
All the little boys and girls,
With rosy cheeks and flaxen curls,
And sparkling eyes and teeth like pearls,
Tripping and skipping, ran merrily after
The wonderful music with shouting and laughter.

The Mayor was dumb, and the Council stood
As if they were changed into blocks of wood,
Unable to move a step, or cry
To the children merrily skipping by
– Could only follow with the eye
That joyous crowd at the Piper's back.
But how the Mayor was on the rack,
And the wretched Council's bosoms beat,
As the Piper turned from the High Street
To where the Weser rolled its waters
Right in the way of their sons and daughters!
However he turned from south to west,
And to Koppelberg Hill his steps addressed,

And after him the children pressed;
Great was the joy in every breast.
'He never can cross that mighty top!
He's forced to let the piping drop,
And we shall see our children stop!'
When, lo, as they reached the mountain-side,
A wondrous portal opened wide,
As if a cavern was suddenly hollowed;
And the Piper advanced and the children followed,
And when all were in to the very last,
The door in the mountain-side shut fast.
Did I say, all? No! One was lame,
    And could not dance the whole of the way;
And in after years, if you would blame
    His sadness, he was used to say –
'It's dull in our town since my playmates left!
I can't forget that I'm bereft
Of all the pleasant sights they see
Which the Piper also promised me.
For he led us, he said, to a joyous land,
Joining the town and just at hand
Where waters gushed and fruit trees grew
And flowers put forth a fairer hue,
And everything was strange and new;
The sparrows were brighter than peacocks here,
And their dogs outran our fallow deer,
And honey-bees had lost their stings,
And horses were born with eagles' wings:
And just as I became assured
My lame foot would be speedily cured,

The music stopped and I stood still,
And found myself outside the hill,
Left alone against my will,
To go now limping as before,
And never hear of that country more!'

|100|

MY LAST DUCHESS
FERRARA

That's my last Duchess painted on the wall,
Looking as if she were alive. I call
That piece a wonder, now: Frà Pandolf's hands
Worked busily a day, and there she stands.
Will't please you sit and look at her? I said
'Frà Pandolf' by design, for never read
Strangers like you that pictured countenance,
The depth and passion of its earnest glance,
But to myself they turned (since none puts by
The curtain I have drawn for you, but I)
And seemed as they would ask me, if they durst,
How such a glance came there; so, not the first
Are you to turn and ask thus. Sir, 'twas not
Her husband's presence only, called that spot
Of joy into the Duchess' cheek: perhaps
Frà Pandolf chanced to say 'Her mantle laps
Over my lady's wrist too much,' or 'Paint
Must never hope to reproduce the faint
Half-flush that dies along her throat:' such stuff
Was courtesy, she thought, and cause enough
For calling up that spot of joy. She had
A heart — how shall I say? — too soon made glad,
Too easily impressed; she liked whate'er
She looked on, and her looks went everywhere.

Sir, 'twas all one! My favour at her breast,
The dropping of the daylight in the West,
The bough of cherries some officious fool
Broke in the orchard for her, the white mule
She rode with round the terrace – all and each
Would draw from her alike the approving speech,
Or blush, at least. She thanked men, – good! but thanked
Somehow – I know not how – as if she ranked
My gift of a nine-hundred-years-old name
With anybody's gift.
                     Oh sir, she smiled, no doubt,
Whene'er I passed her; but who passed without
Much the same smile? This grew; I gave commands;
Then all smiles stopped together. There she stands
As if alive. Will't please you rise? We'll meet
The company below then. I repeat,
The Count your master's known munificence
Is ample warrant that no just pretence
Of mine for dowry will be disallowed;
Though his fair daughter's self, as I avowed
At starting, is my object. Nay, we'll go
Together down, sir.

ROBERT BURNS
1759–96

Burns was born on 25 January 1759 in Alloway, Ayrshire, the eldest of seven children of a gardener who was determined that his son should have as good an education as possible in their straitened circumstances. The young Burns read avidly – he was well versed in the classics – and began to write poetry as a schoolboy. After the death of their father in 1784, Burns and his brother Gilbert tried their hand at farming but without success. Robert was on the point of emigrating to Jamaica when the publication of his poetry in 1786 and the excitement which it generated caused him to change his mind. He visited Edinburgh, where he was lionised by fashionable society, and through his association with the Scots Musical Museum he came to write the words of many of the traditional Scottish songs known today. An inveterate womaniser, he married Jean Armour in 1786 but continued to have affairs and father a number of children outside wedlock. He joined the Excise Service in 1789 and moved to Dumfries. Originally a passionate supporter of the French Revolution, he took up arms against France by joining the Dumfries Volunteers in 1795.

He died on 21 July 1796, of heart disease brought on by rheumatic fever. In 1885 a bust of Burns was erected in Westminster Abbey, financed by a number of patriotic

Scots, each of whom contributed a shilling. Every Burns Night, 25 January, his life and work are still celebrated with great ceremony all over the world.

Robert Burns

TO A MOUSE

Wee sleeket, cow'rin', tim'rous beastie,
O, what a panic's in thy breastie!
Thou need na start awa' sae hasty,
     Wi' bickerin' brattle!
I wad be laith to rin an' chase thee
     Wi' murderin' pattle!

I'm truly sorry man's dominion,
Has broken nature's social union,
An' justifies that ill opinion,
     Which makes thee startle
At me, thy poor, earth-born companion,
     An' fellow-mortal!

I doubt na, whyles, but thou may thieve;
What then? poor beastie, thou maun live!
A daimen icker in a thrave
     'S a sma' request;
I'll get a blessin' wi' the lave,
     An' never miss't!

Thy wee bit housie, too, in ruin!
Its silly wa's the win's are strewin'!
An' naething, now, to big a new ane,
          O' foggage green!
An' bleak December's winds ensuin',
              Baith snell an' keen!

Thou saw the fields laid bare an' waste,
An' weary winter comin' fast,
An' cozie here, beneath the blast,
          Thou thought to dwell –
Till crash! the cruel coulter past
            Out thro' thy cell.

That wee bit heap o' leaves an' stibble,
Has cost thee mony a weary nibble!
Now thou's turn'd out, for a' thy trouble,
          But house or hald,
To thole the winter's sleety dribble,
            An' crancreuch cauld!

But Mousie, thou art no thy lane,
In proving foresight may be vain;
The best-laid schemes o' mice an' men
          Gang aft agley,
An' lea'e us nought but grief an' pain,
            For promis'd joy!

Still thou art blest, compar'd wi' me!
The present only toucheth thee:
But och! I backward cast my e'e,
       On prospects drear!
An' forward, tho' I canna see,
       I guess an' fear!

81

A RED, RED ROSE

O my Luve's like a red, red rose,
   That's newly sprung in June;
O my Luve's like the melodie
   That's sweetly play'd in tune.

As fair art thou, my bonie lass,
   So deep in luve am I;
And I will luve thee still, my Dear,
   Till a' the seas gang dry.

Till a' the seas gang dry, my Dear,
   And the rocks melt wi' the sun:
And I will luve thee still, my Dear,
   While the sands o' life shall run.

And fare thee weel, my only Luve,
   And fare thee weel a while!
And I will come again, my Luve,
   Tho' it were ten thousand mile!

Robert Burns

From TAM O'SHANTER

Warlocks and witches in a dance:
Nae cotillion, brent new frae France,
But hornpipes, jigs, strathspeys, and reels,
Put life and mettle in their heels.
A winnock-bunker in the east,
There sat Auld Nick, in shape o' beast;
A towzie tyke, black, grim, and large,
To gie them music was his charge:
He screw'd the pipes and gart them skirl,
Till roof and rafters a' did dirl.
Coffins stood round, like open presses,
That shaw'd the dead in their last dresses;
And, by some devilish cantraip sleight,
Each in its cauld hand held a light:
By which heroic Tam was able
To note upon the haly table,
A murderer's banes, in gibbet-airns;
Twa span-lang, wee, unchristen'd bairns;
A thief new-cutted frae a rape –
Wi' his last gasp his gab did gape;
Five tomahawks wi' bluid red-rusted;
Five scymitars wi' murder crusted;
A garter which a babe had strangled;
A knife a father's throat had mangled –
Whom his ain son o' life bereft –

The grey hairs yet stack to the heft;
Wi' mair of horrible and awefu',
Which even to name wad be unlawfu'.

    As Tammie glowr'd, amaz'd, and curious,
The mirth and fun grew fast and furious;
The piper loud and louder blew,
The dancers quick and quicker flew,
They reel'd, they set, they cross'd, they cleekit,
Till ilka carlin swat and reekit,
And coost her duddies to the wark,
And linket at it in her sark!

* * *

    But here my Muse her wing maun cour,
Sic flights as far beyond her pow'r:
To sing how Nannie lap and flang
(A souple jade she was and strang),
And how Tam stood like ane bewitch'd,
And thought his very een enrich'd;
Even Satan glowr'd, and fidg'd fu' fain,
And hotch'd and blew wi' might and main;
Till first ae caper, syne anither,
Tam tint his reason a' thegither,
And roars out: 'Weel done, Cutty-sark!'
And in an instant all was dark;
And scarcely had he Maggie rallied,
When out the hellish legion sallied.

Robert Burns

As beez bizz out wi' angry fyke,
When plundering herds assail their byke;
As open pussie's mortal foes,
When, pop! she starts before their nose;
As eager runs the market-crowd,
When 'Catch the thief' resounds aloud:
So Maggie runs, the witches follow,
Wi' mony an eldritch skreech and hollow.

LORD BYRON
1788–1824

George Gordon, Lord Byron, was born in London on 22 January 1788, the son of an unprincipled womaniser and spendthrift who died when his son was three. His mother, who behaved towards the boy with either passionate devotion or physical violence, took him to Aberdeen where they lived in humble circumstances. On the death of a dissolute uncle, both the title of Lord Byron and Newstead Abbey, the family home, passed to the eleven-year-old boy. After an operation to strengthen his feet (he had been born with a club foot) the 6th Lord Byron attended school in Dulwich before going to Harrow and Trinity College, Cambridge.

From 1811 he travelled widely in the Mediterranean, and his visit to Greece made him a passionate supporter of Greek independence from the Ottoman Empire. By now he was a celebrity described as 'mad, bad and dangerous to know', his fame spread as much by his notorious behaviour with a string of mistresses as by his poetry. He fathered children by three women and then ran off with the Countess Guiccioli, with whom he lived openly in Pisa. In January 1824 Byron sailed to Greece to take part in the revolt against Turkish rule. Three months later, on 19 April, he died of fever, but his scandalous reputation survived him. Neither the Dean of Westminster Abbey nor the Dean of

St Paul's would allow the body to be buried under their church roofs and, after lying in state in London for several days, it was buried in the Byron family vault near Newstead.

65

SHE WALKS IN BEAUTY

She walks in beauty, like the night
   Of cloudless climes and starry skies;
And all that's best of dark and bright
   Meet in her aspect and her eyes:
Thus mellow'd to that tender light
   Which heaven to gaudy day denies.

One shade the more, one ray the less,
   Had half impair'd the nameless grace
Which waves in every raven tress,
   Or softly lightens o'er her face;
Where thoughts serenely sweet express
   How pure, how dear their dwelling-place.

And on that cheek, and o'er that brow,
   So soft, so calm, yet eloquent,
The smiles that win, the tints that glow,
   But tell of days in goodness spent,
A mind at peace with all below,
   A heart whose love is innocent!

LEWIS CARROLL
1832–98

—— ఆసిసిసి ——

Lewis Carroll was the pseudonym of Charles Dodgson who was born at Daresbury near Warrington on 27 January 1832, the son of a clergyman. At the age of eleven he moved with his family to Croft in North Yorkshire. Carroll was educated at Rugby and at Christ Church, Oxford, and from an early age was fascinated by writing.

In 1855 Carroll took up a post as Lecturer in Mathematics at Christ Church. On a picnic on the banks of the Thames with the daughter of the Dean, Dr Liddell, he began to spin the tale which was to turn into *Alice's Adventures in Wonderland*. Carroll used Alice Liddell, one of the daughters, as the model for the central character in the story. When published, with illustrations by Sir John Tenniel, the book became so popular that a sequel, *Through the Looking-Glass and what Alice found there*, followed in 1871. Carroll continued to produce mathematical treatises, narrative poems and short stories, dying in Guildford on 14 January 1898.

'Jabberwocky' originated in a game of verse-making when Carroll was staying with some cousins in 1855, although he had written the first verse seventeen years earlier. In the early 1890s a school wrote to Carroll asking if they might call their new magazine 'Jabberwok'. Carroll agreed, pointing out that the Anglo-Saxon word *wocer* means 'offspring' or 'fruit', while *jabber* means 'an excited or voluble discussion', making it an ideal title for a magazine.

54

JABBERWOCKY

'Twas brillig, and the slithy toves
  Did gyre and gimble in the wabe;
All mimsy were the borogroves,
  And the mome raths outgrabe.

'Beware the Jabberwock, my son!
  The jaws that bite, the claws that catch!
Beware the Jubjub bird, and shun
  The frumious Bandersnatch!'

He took his vorpal sword in hand:
  Long time the manxome foe he sought –
So rested he by the Tumtum tree,
  And stood awhile in thought.

And as in uffish thought he stood,
  The Jabberwock, with eyes of flame,
Came whiffling through the tulgey wood,
  And burbled as it came!

One, two! One, two! And through and through
  The vorpal blade went snicker-snack!
He left it dead, and with its head
  He went galumphing back.

'And thou hast slain the Jabberwock?
   Come to my arms, my beamish boy!
O frabjous day! Callooh! Callay!'
   He chortled in his joy.

'Twas brillig, and the slithy toves
   Did gyre and gimble in the wabe;
All mimsy were the borogroves,
   And the mome raths outgrabe.

G. K. CHESTERTON
1874–1936

Gilbert Keith Chesterton was born in Kensington, West London, on 29 May 1874, the son of an estate agent. He attended St Paul's School, then enrolled at the Slade School of Art before reading English Literature at London University, which he left without taking a degree. He began his career as a journalist by contributing to the *Spectator*, and was already a well-known figure when his opposition to the Boer War brought him into contact with Hilaire Belloc and the two became close friends. They shared a distaste for, amongst other things, women's suffrage and agnosticism, which brought them into conflict with such notables as Shaw and H. G. Wells. In 1905 Chesterton began a weekly column for the *Illustrated London News* which ran, virtually without interruption, until 1930.

A large man, Chesterton seemed to grow more out-sized and more absent-minded every year. On one famous occasion, on his way to give one of his many talks, he telegraphed his wife with the plea: 'Am in Market Harborough – where ought I to be?' For all the essays, poems and articles which poured from his pen, Chesterton is probably best remembered for the creation of the clerical sleuth Father Brown. When he died at his home in Beaconsfield, Buckinghamshire, on 14 June 1936, Belloc observed that 'Chesterton will never occur again'.

36

THE DONKEY

When fishes flew and forests walked
   And figs grew upon thorn,
Some moment when the moon was blood
   Then surely I was born.

With monstrous head and sickening cry
   And ears like errant wings,
The devil's walking parody
   On all four-footed things.

The tattered outlaw of the earth,
   Of ancient crooked will;
Starve, scourge, deride me: I am dumb,
   I keep my secret still.

Fools! For I also had my hour;
   One far fierce hour and sweet:
There was a shout about my ears,
   And palms before my feet.

87

From LEPANTO

White founts falling in the courts of the sun,
And the Soldan of Byzantium is smiling as they run;
There is laughter like the fountains in that face of all
  men feared,
It stirs the forest darkness, the darkness of his beard,
It curls the blood-red crescent, the crescent of his lips,
For the inmost sea of all the earth is shaken with his ships.
They have dared the white republics up the capes of Italy,
They have dashed the Adriatic round the Lion of the Sea,
And the Pope has cast his arms abroad for agony and loss,
And called the kings of Christendom for swords about the
  Cross,
The cold queen of England is looking in the glass;
The shadow of the Valois is yawning at the Mass;
From evening isles fantastical rings faint the Spanish gun,
And the Lord upon the Golden Horn is laughing in the sun.

Dim drums throbbing, in the hills half heard,
Where only on a nameless throne a crownless prince has
  stirred,
Where, risen from a doubtful seat and half-attainted stall,
The last knight of Europe takes weapons from the wall,
The last and lingering troubadour to whom the bird has
  sung,

That once went singing southward when all the world was
   young,
In that enormous silence, tiny and unafraid,
Comes up along a winding road the noise of the Crusade.
Strong gongs groaning as the guns boom far,
Don John of Austria is going to the war,
Stiff flags straining in the night-blasts cold
In the gloom black-purple, in the glint old-gold,
Torchlight crimson on the copper kettle-drums,
Then the tuckets, then the trumpets, then the cannon, and
   he comes.
Don John laughing in the brave beard curled,
Spurning of his stirrups like the thrones of all the world,
Holding his head up for a flag of all the free.
Love-light of Spain – hurrah!
Death-light of Africa!
Don John of Austria
Is riding to the sea.

ARTHUR HUGH CLOUGH
1819–61

Clough was born in Liverpool on 1 January 1819, the son of a cotton merchant who took his family with him to South Carolina four years later. The boy was sent back to England in 1828 to go to school at Rugby, where the famous Dr Arnold was headmaster. Thanks to his academic gifts Clough became a favourite of Arnold's, who created the position of Head of School for him and held him up as an example to other pupils. At Balliol College, Oxford, Clough's precocious talents seemed to desert him. After gaining only second-class honours, he walked the fifty miles to Rugby to confess to his old mentor that he'd 'failed'.

This seemed to set the tone for his subsequent short life. He lost in a competition for a fellowship at Balliol, having to be satisfied with one at the less prestigious Oriel College. He resigned in 1848 to take part in the revolutionary movement which was sweeping the capitals of Europe, and joined Mazzini's forces in Italy. Back in London, he took up a post as Professor of English at University College, but resigned in 1852 in protest against the rigidity of the Unitarians who owned the institution. He married a cousin of Florence Nightingale's and joined her in lobbying for the reform of hospitals and the medical profession. He died in Florence on 13 November 1861, aged only forty-two.

91

SAY NOT THE STRUGGLE NOUGHT AVAILETH

Say not the struggle nought availeth,
　The labour and the wounds are vain,
The enemy faints not, nor faileth,
　And as things have been they remain.

If hopes were dupes, fears may be liars;
　It may be, in yon smoke conceal'd,
Your comrades chase e'en now the fliers,
　And, but for you, possess the field.

For while the tired waves, vainly breaking,
　Seem here no painful inch to gain,
Far back, through creeks and inlets making,
　Comes silent, flooding in, the main,

And not by eastern windows only,
　When daylight comes, comes in the light,
In front, the sun climbs slow, how slowly,
　But westward, look, the land is bright.

SAMUEL TAYLOR COLERIDGE
1772–1834

Coleridge was born on 24 October 1772, the youngest of thirteen children of the Vicar of Ottery St Mary in Devon. Aged seven, the young Coleridge was sent to Christ's Hospital, where his fellow-pupils included the future essayist Charles Lamb. Coleridge detested the place and admitted that 'from eight to fourteen I was a playless day-dreamer and idler'. Yet he defied jaundice and rheumatic fever to become a good classical scholar and went up to Jesus College, Cambridge, in 1791. Later he tried his luck as a soldier and then, with the poet Robert Southey, dreamt of becoming a settler and founding an idealistic colony in America.

Thanks to the financial support of a Bristol poet and bookseller, Coleridge was able to move to Nether Stowey in the Quantock Hills where his output included 'The Rime of the Ancient Mariner'. While there he received such leading literary figures as Wordsworth and Hazlitt. But by now he was becoming increasingly addicted to opium; his own efforts and those of his friends to break the habit were in vain. Both 'The Rime of the Ancient Mariner' and 'Kubla Khan' were written under the influence of the drug. Coleridge died on 25 July 1834.

25

THE RIME OF THE ANCIENT MARINER

PART I

It is an ancient Mariner,
And he stoppeth one of three.
'By thy long grey beard and glittering eye,
Now wherefore stopp'st thou me?

The Bridegroom's doors are opened wide,
And I am next of kin;
The guests are met, the feast is set:
May'st hear the merry din.'

He holds him with his skinny hand,
'There was a ship,' quoth he.
'Hold off: unhand me, greybeard loon!'
Eftsoons his hand dropt he.

He holds him with his glittering eye –
The Wedding-Guest stood still,
And listens like a three years' child:
The Mariner hath his will.

The Wedding-Guest sat on a stone:
He cannot choose but hear;
And thus spake on that ancient man,
The bright-eyed Mariner.

'The ship was cheered, the harbour cleared,
Merrily did we drop
Below the kirk, below the hill,
Below the lighthouse top.

The Sun came up upon the left,
Out of the sea came he!
And he shone bright, and on the right
Went down into the sea.

Higher and higher every day,
Till over the mast at noon – '
The Wedding-Guest here beat his breast,
For he heard the loud bassoon.

The bride hath paced into the hall,
Red as a rose is she;
Nodding their heads before her goes
The merry minstrelsy.

The Wedding-Guest he beat his breast,
Yet he cannot choose but hear;
And thus spake on that ancient man,
The bright-eyed Mariner.

'And now the Storm-blast came, and he
Was tyrannous and strong:
He struck with his o'ertaking wings,
And chased us south along.

With sloping masts and dipping prow,
As who pursued with yell and blow
Still treads the shadow of his foe,
And forward bends his head,
The ship drove fast, loud roared the blast,
And southward aye we fled.

And now there came both mist and snow,
And it grew wondrous cold:
And ice, mast-high, came floating by,
As green as emerald.

And through the drifts the snowy clifts
Did send a dismal sheen:
Nor shapes of men nor beasts we ken –
The ice was all between.

The ice was here, the ice was there,
The ice was all around:
It cracked and growled, and roared and howled,
Like noises in a swound!

At length did cross an Albatross,
Thorough the fog it came;
As if it had been a Christian soul,
We hailed it in God's name.

It ate the food it ne'er had eat,
And round and round it flew.
The ice did split with a thunder-fit;
The helmsman steered us through!

And a good south wind sprung up behind;
The Albatross did follow,
And every day, for food or play,
Came to the mariner's hollo!

In mist or cloud, on mast or shroud,
It perched for vespers nine;
Whiles all the night, through fog-smoke white,
Glimmered the white Moon-shine.'

'God save thee, ancient Mariner!
From the fiends, that plague thee thus! –
Why look'st thou so?' – 'With my cross-bow
I shot the Albatross!'

35

KUBLA KHAN

In Xanadu did Kubla Khan
A stately pleasure-dome decree:
Where Alph, the sacred river, ran
Through caverns measureless to man
  Down to a sunless sea.
So twice five miles of fertile ground
With walls and towers were girdled round:
And there were gardens bright with sinuous rills,
Where blossomed many an incense-bearing tree;
And here were forests ancient as the hills,
Enfolding sunny spots of greenery.

But oh! that deep romantic chasm which slanted
Down the green hill athwart a cedarn cover!
A savage place! as holy and enchanted
As e'er beneath a waning moon was haunted
By woman wailing for her demon-lover!
And from this chasm, with ceaseless turmoil seething,
As if this earth in fast thick pants were breathing,
A mighty fountain momently was forced:
Amid whose swift half-intermitted burst
Huge fragments vaulted like rebounding hail,
Or chaffy grain beneath the thresher's flail:
And 'mid these dancing rocks at once and ever
It flung up momently the sacred river.

Five miles meandering with a mazy motion
Through wood and dale the sacred river ran,
Then reached the caverns measureless to man,
And sank in tumult to a lifeless ocean:
And 'mid this tumult Kubla heard from far
Ancestral voices prophesying war!

The shadow of the dome of pleasure
Floated midway on the waves;
Where was heard the mingled measure
From the fountain and the caves.
It was a miracle of rare device,
A sunny pleasure-dome with caves of ice!

A damsel with a dulcimer
In a vision once I saw:
It was an Abyssinian maid,
And on her dulcimer she played,
Singing of Mount Abora.
Could I revive within me
Her symphony and song,
To such a deep delight 'twould win me,
That with music loud and long,
I would build that dome in air,
That sunny dome! those caves of ice!
And all who heard should see them there,
And all should cry, 'Beware! Beware!
His flashing eyes, his floating hair!
Weave a circle round him thrice,

And close your eyes with holy dread,
  For he on honey-dew hath fed,
  And drunk the milk of Paradise.'

W. H. DAVIES
1871–1940

———— ∞ ————

William Henry Davies was born in Newport, Monmouth-shire, on either 25 April 1871, according to his own account, or on 3 July 1871, according to his birth certificate. After his father's death and his mother's remarriage, Davies and his siblings were brought up by their grandparents. At school he discovered a liking for poetry and, after abandoning his apprenticeship as a picture-framer, went to try his luck in America. There he became a hobo, leading a nomadic existence, riding freight cars, working in the fruit-fields and narrowly escaping with his life after an attack of malaria and an assault by armed robbers. He joined the Gold Rush to the Klondike in the company of the wonderfully named Three-Fingered Jack, but slipped when trying to jump on to a moving freight train and subsequently lost a leg.

Back in London, he lived in a hostel for down-and-outs in Blackfriars, but his poetry began to attract attention, championed by Shaw and Edward Thomas. In 1923, at the age of fifty-two, he married a nurse half his age. He died at Nailsworth in Gloucestershire on 26 September 1940. Of his enormous output, 'Leisure' is probably the best remembered.

11

LEISURE

What is this life if, full of care,
We have no time to stand and stare?

No time to stand beneath the boughs
And stare as long as sheep or cows.

No time to see, when woods we pass,
Where squirrels hide their nuts in grass.

No time to see, in broad daylight,
Streams full of stars, like skies at night.

No time to turn at Beauty's glance,
And watch her feet, how they can dance.

No time to wait till her mouth can
Enrich that smile her eyes began.

A poor life this if, full of care,
We have no time to stand and stare.

WALTER DE LA MARE
1873–1956

Born in Charlton, Kent, in 1873, Walter de la Mare was the son of a Bank of England official and related through his mother to Robert Browning. Educated at St Paul's Cathedral Choir School, where he founded the *Choristers' Journal*, he worked for twenty years for the Standard Oil Company as a clerk until Sir Henry Newbolt used his influence to secure De la Mare a Civil List pension of £100 a year.

He soon built up a formidable reputation, writing for both adults and children in his unique style. In company with Rupert Brooke and Wilfrid Gibson he contributed to the first volume of *Georgian Poetry*. As a beneficiary of Brooke's will he was able to concentrate on his literary career, returning the favour by writing a critical study of Brooke as well as similar works on Lewis Carroll and Christina Rossetti. He was created a Companion of Honour and then awarded the Order of Merit in 1953. He died on 22 June 1956.

3

THE LISTENERS

'Is there anybody there?' said the Traveller,
   Knocking on the moonlit door;
And his horse in the silence champed the grasses
   Of the forest's ferny floor:
And a bird flew up out of the turret,
   Above the Traveller's head:
And he smote upon the door again a second time;
   'Is there anybody there?' he said.
But no one descended to the Traveller;
   No head from the leaf-fringed sill
Leaned over and looked into his grey eyes,
   Where he stood perplexed and still.
But only a host of phantom listeners
   That dwelt in the lone house then
Stood listening in the quiet of the moonlight
   To that voice from the world of men:
Stood thronging the faint moonbeams on the dark stair,
   That goes down to the empty hall,
Hearkening in an air stirred and shaken
   By the lonely Traveller's call.
And he felt in his heart their strangeness,
   Their stillness answering his cry,
While his horse moved, cropping the dark turf,
   'Neath the starred and leafy sky;
For he suddenly smote on the door, even

Louder, and lifted his head: –
'Tell them I came, and no one answered,
    That I kept my word,' he said.
Never the least stir made the listeners,
    Though every word he spake
Fell echoing through the shadowiness of the still house
    From the one man left awake:
Ay, they heard his foot upon the stirrup,
    And the sound of iron on stone,
And how the silence surged softly backward,
    When the plunging hoofs were gone.

49

SILVER

Slowly, silently, now the moon
Walks the night in her silver shoon;
This way, and that, she peers, and sees
Silver fruit upon silver trees;
One by one the casements catch
Her beams beneath the silvery thatch;
Couched in his kennel, like a log,
With paws of silver sleeps the dog;
From their shadowy cote the white breasts peep
Of doves in a silver-feathered sleep;
A harvest mouse goes scampering by,
With silver claws, and silver eye;
And moveless fish in the water gleam,
By silver reeds in a silver stream.

JOHN DONNE
1572–1631

Donne was born in London into a staunchly Catholic
family. His religion barred him from taking a degree, but
in May 1592 he abjured his Catholic faith to become a law
student at Lincoln's Inn. In 1596 he sailed with the Earl of
Essex on the voyage to sack Cadiz, and the following year
joined Sir Walter Raleigh on a raid against Spanish treasure
ships off the Azores. He was already writing poems about
his adventures when he joined the service of Sir Thomas
Egerton, Lord Keeper of the Great Seal, whose niece, Anne,
Donne secretly married. When the marriage was discovered, Donne was briefly jailed in the Fleet Prison. After his
release he was taken into the protection of Sir Francis
Wooley, who installed Donne at Pyrford Manor by the River
Wey where he continued to write. Other powerful friends
ensured that he was restored to official favour, and in 1610
he was awarded an honorary MA by Oxford University. It
was James I who suggested that Donne take up holy orders,
forcing Cambridge University to create him a Doctor of
Divinity. It was the patronage of George Villiers, Duke of
Buckingham, which enabled Donne to become Dean of
St Paul's for the last decade of his life. Donne died on 31
March 1631.

69

THE GOOD-MORROW

I wonder by my troth, what thou, and I
  Did, till we lov'd? were we not wean'd till then?
But suck'd on countrey pleasures, childishly?
  Or snorted we in the seven sleepers' den?
'Twas so; but this, all pleasures fancies bee;
If ever any beauty I did see,
Which I desir'd, and got, 'twas but a dreame of thee.

And now good morrow to our waking soules,
  Which watch not one another out of feare;
For love, all love of other sights controules,
  And makes one little roome an every where.
Let sea-discoverers to new worlds have gone,
Let maps to others, worlds on worlds have showne,
Let us possesse one world, each hath one, and is one.

My face in thine eye, thine in mine appeares,
  And true plaine hearts doe in the faces rest,
Where can we finde two better hemispheares
  Without sharpe North, without declining West?
What ever dyes, was not mixt equally;
If our two loves be one, or thou and I
Love so alike, that none doe slacken, none can die.

John Donne

A VALEDICTION: FORBIDDING MOURNING

As virtuous men passe mildly away,
 And whisper to their soules, to goe,
Whilst some of their sad friends doe say,
 The breath goes now, and some say, no:

So let us melt, and make no noise,
 No teare-floods, nor sigh-tempests move,
'Twere prophanation of our joyes
 To tell the layetie our love.

Moving of th' earth brings harmes and feares,
 Men reckon what it did and meant,
But trepidation of the spheares,
 Though greater farre, is innocent.

Dull sublunary lovers' love
 (Whose soule is sense) cannot admit
Absence, because it doth remove
 Those things which elemented it.

But we by a love, so much refin'd,
 That our selves know not what it is,
Inter-assured of the mind,
 Care lesse, eyes, lips, and hands to misse.

Our two soules therefore, which are one,
    Though I must goe, endure not yet
A breach, but an expansion,
    Like gold to ayery thinnesse beate.

If they be two, they are two so
    As stiffe twin compasses are two,
Thy soule the fixt foot, makes no show
    To move, but doth, if th'other doe.

And though it in the centre sit,
    Yet when the other far doth rome,
It leanes, and hearkens after it,
    And growes erect, as that comes home.

Such wilt thou be to mee, who must
    Like th'other foot, obliquely runne;
Thy firmness makes my circle just,
    And makes me end, where I begunne.

T. S. ELIOT
1888–1965

Thomas Stearns Eliot was born in St Louis, Missouri, on 26 September 1888, the seventh and last child of a wealthy businessman. By the turn of the century, the family had acquired a summer home in Massachusetts. In 1906 Eliot went up to Harvard. He also studied at the Sorbonne in Paris and at the University of Marburg in Germany, and in 1914 he arrived in Britain to continue his studies at Merton College, Oxford. He wrote poetry while earning a living as a schoolmaster: one of his pupils at Highgate School in North London was the young John Betjeman, who presented Eliot with some of his very early works.

At the suggestion of his fellow expatriate poet, Ezra Pound, Eliot decided to settle in England, and in the summer of 1915 he married Vivien Haigh-Wood. Two years later he joined Lloyds Bank, from which he was rescued by the efforts of supporters such as Virginia Woolf, who secured him a job at the publishers Faber and Faber. He was therefore in a position to nurture several of the younger British poets, notably Spender and Auden, whose work he introduced to the Faber list.

In 1927 Eliot became a British citizen and announced his conversion to Anglo-Catholicism. A few years later he and his wife officially separated after a marriage blighted by her uncertain mental state – the subject of Michael Hastings' play *Tom and Viv* which was recently filmed with Miranda Richardson and Willem Dafoe in the title roles. After the Second World War Eliot turned to the theatre, writing poetic dramas such as *The Cocktail Party* and *The Family Reunion*. In 1965, the year of his death, he was awarded the Order of Merit and the Nobel Prize for Literature, and he has found unlikely popular posthumous fame on the West End musical stage. In 1981 *Cats*, the Andrew Lloyd Webber musical based on Eliot's 1939 *Old Possum's Book of Practical Cats* (from which 'Macavity: The Mystery Cat' is included here), opened at the New London Theatre, and it has played to packed houses ever since.

30

JOURNEY OF THE MAGI

'A cold coming we had of it.
Just the worst time of the year
For a journey, and such a long journey:
The ways deep and the weather sharp,
The very dead of winter.'
And the camels galled, sore-footed, refractory,
Lying down in the melting snow.
There were times we regretted
The summer palaces on slopes, the terraces,
And the silken girls bringing sherbet.
Then the camel men cursing and grumbling
And running away, and wanting their liquor and women,
And the night-fires going out, and the lack of shelters,
And the cities hostile and the towns unfriendly
And the villages dirty and charging high prices:
A hard time we had of it.
At the end we preferred to travel all night,
Sleeping in snatches,
With the voices singing in our ears, saying
That this was all folly.

Then at dawn we came down to a temperate valley,
Wet, below the snow line, smelling of vegetation,
With a running stream and a water-mill beating the
  darkness,

And three trees on the low sky.
And an old white horse galloped away in the meadow.
Then we came to a tavern with vine-leaves over the lintel,
Six hands at an open door dicing for pieces of silver,
And feet kicking the empty wine-skins.
But there was no information, and so we continued
And arrived at evening, not a moment too soon
Finding the place; it was (you may say) satisfactory.

   All this was a long time ago, I remember,
And I would do it again, but set down
This set down
This: were we led all that way for
Birth or Death? There was a Birth, certainly,
We had evidence and no doubt. I had seen birth and death,
But had thought they were different; this Birth was
Hard and bitter agony for us, like Death, our death.
We returned to our places, these Kingdoms,
But no longer at ease here, in the old dispensation,
With an alien people clutching their gods.
I should be glad of another death.

68

MACAVITY: THE MYSTERY CAT

Macavity's a Mystery Cat: he's called the Hidden Paw –
For he's the master criminal who can defy the Law.
He's the bafflement of Scotland Yard, the Flying Squad's
  despair:
For when they reach the scene of crime – *Macavity's not
  there*!

Macavity, Macavity, there's no one like Macavity,
He's broken every human law, he breaks the law of gravity.
His powers of levitation would make a fakir stare,
And when you reach the scene of crime – *Macavity's not
  there*!
You may seek him in the basement, you may look up in the
  air –
But I tell you once and once again, *Macavity's not there*!

Macavity's a ginger cat, he's very tall and thin;
You would know him if you saw him, for his eyes are
  sunken in.
His brow is deeply lined with thought, his head is highly
  domed;
His coat is dusty from neglect, his whiskers are uncombed.
He sways his head from side to side, with movements like
  a snake;
And when you think he's half asleep, he's always wide
  awake.

Macavity, Macavity, there's no one like Macavity,
For he's a fiend in feline shape, a monster of depravity.
You may meet him in a by-street, you may see him in the
    square –
But when a crime's discovered, then *Macavity's not there*!

He's outwardly respectable. (They say he cheats at cards.)
And his footprints are not found in any file of Scotland
    Yard's.
And when the larder's looted, or the jewel-case is rifled,
Or when the milk is missing, or another Peke's been stifled,
Or the greenhouse glass is broken, and the trellis past
    repair –
Ay, there's the wonder of the thing! *Macavity's not there*!

And when the Foreign Office find a Treaty's gone astray,
Or the Admiralty lose some plans and drawings by the
    way,
There may be a scrap of paper in the hall or on the stair –
But it's useless to investigate – *Macavity's not there*!
And when the loss has been disclosed, the Secret Service
    say:
'It *must* have been Macavity!' – but he's a mile away.
You'll be sure to find him resting, or a-licking of his
    thumbs,
Or engaged in doing complicated long division sums.

Macavity, Macavity, there's no one like Macavity,
There never was a Cat of such deceitfulness and suavity.
He always has an alibi, and one or two to spare:

T. S. Eliot

At whatever time the deed took place – MACAVITY WASN'T
   THERE!
And they say that all the Cats whose wicked deeds are
   widely known
(I might mention Mungojerrie, I might mention
   Griddlebone)
Are nothing more than agents for the Cat who all the time
Just controls their operations: the Napoleon of Crime!

88

THE WASTE LAND

PART I: THE BURIAL OF THE DEAD

April is the cruellest month, breeding
Lilacs out of the dead land, mixing
Memory and desire, stirring
Dull roots with spring rain.
Winter kept us warm, covering
Earth in forgetful snow, feeding
A little life with dried tubers.
Summer surprised us, coming over the Starnbergersee
With a shower of rain; we stopped in the colonnade,
And went on in sunlight, into the Hofgarten,
And drank coffee, and talked for an hour.
Bin gar keine Russin, stamm' aus Litauen, echt deutsch.
And when we were children, staying at the arch-duke's,
My cousin's, he took me out on a sled,
And I was frightened. He said, Marie,
Marie, hold on tight. And down we went.
In the mountains, there you feel free.
I read, much of the night, and go south in the winter.

What are the roots that clutch, what branches grow
Out of this stony rubbish? Son of man,
You cannot say, or guess, for you know only
A heap of broken images, where the sun beats,
And the dead tree gives no shelter, the cricket no relief,

And the dry stone no sound of water. Only
There is shadow under this red rock,
(Come in under the shadow of this red rock),
And I will show you something different from either
Your shadow at morning striding behind you
Or your shadow at evening rising to meet you;
I will show you fear in a handful of dust.

> *Frisch weht der Wind*
> *Der Heimat zu*
> *Mein Irisch Kind*
> *Wo weilest du?*

'You gave me hyacinths first a year ago;
'They called me the hyacinth girl.'
– Yet when we came back, late, from the hyacinth garden,
Your arms were full, and your hair wet, I could not
Speak, and my eyes failed, I was neither
Living nor dead, and I knew nothing,
Looking into the heart of light, the silence.
Oed' und leer das Meer.

   Madame Sosostris, famous clairvoyante,
Had a bad cold, nevertheless
Is known to be the wisest woman in Europe,
With a wicked pack of cards. Here, said she,
Is your card, the drowned Phoenician Sailor,
(Those are pearls that were his eyes. Look!)
Here is Belladonna, the Lady of the Rocks,
The lady of situations,
Here is the man with three staves, and here the Wheel,
And here is the one-eyed merchant, and this card,

Which is blank, is something he carries on his back,
Which I am forbidden to see. I do not find
The Hanged Man. Fear death by water.
I see crowds of people, walking round in a ring.
Thank you. If you see dear Mrs Equitone,
Tell her I bring the horoscope myself:
One must be so careful these days.

  Unreal City,
Under the brown fog of a winter dawn,
A crowd flowed over London Bridge, so many,
I had not thought death had undone so many.
Sighs, short and infrequent, were exhaled,
And each man fixed his eyes before his feet.
Flowed up the hill and down King William Street,
To where Saint Mary Woolnoth kept the hours
With a dead sound on the final stroke of nine.
There I saw one I knew, and stopped him, crying: 'Stetson!
'You who were with me in the ships at Mylae!
'That corpse you planted last year in your garden,
'Has it begun to sprout? Will it bloom this year?
'Or has the sudden frost disturbed its bed?
'O keep the Dog far hence, that's friend to men,
'Or with his nails he'll dig it up again!
'You! hypocrite lecteur! – mon semblable, – mon frère!'

EDWARD FITZGERALD
1809–83

FitzGerald was born on 31 March 1809 at the Suffolk estate of his Irish landowning family. He was educated at the King Edward VI Grammar School in Bury St Edmunds before going up to Trinity College, Cambridge, where his friends included Thackeray and Tennyson. FitzGerald became Tennyson's patron, granting him an annual gift of £300 for many years.

A man of independent means, FitzGerald settled in Suffolk where his predominantly homosexual tastes led him into close friendships with younger men. It was one of these intimates, Edward Cowell, who sparked FitzGerald's interest in collating and translating the Persian *Rubáiyát of Omar Khayyám.* FitzGerald adapted the source material so freely that it could almost be regarded as his own work, and in any case there must be some doubt whether all of the original can safely be attributed to Khayyám (1048–1131).

FitzGerald died on 14 June 1883 at the house of George Crabbe, son of the poet of the same name.

62

From THE RUBAIYAT OF OMAR KHAYYAM

Awake! for Morning in the Bowl of Night
Has flung the Stone that puts the Stars to Flight:
    And Lo! the Hunter of the East has caught
The Sultan's Turret in a Noose of Light.

Dreaming when Dawn's Left Hand was in the Sky
I heard a Voice within the Tavern cry,
    'Awake, my Little ones, and fill the Cup
'Before Life's Liquor in its Cup be dry.'

And, as the Cock crew, those who stood before
The Tavern shouted – 'Open then the Door!
    'You know how little while we have to stay,
'And, once departed, may return no more.'

Now the New Year reviving old Desires,
The thoughtful Soul to Solitude retires,
    Where the WHITE HAND OF MOSES on the Bough
Puts out, and Jesus from the Ground suspires.

Iram indeed is gone with all its Rose,
And Jamshyd's Sev'n-ring'd Cup where no one knows;
    But still the Vine her ancient Ruby yields,
And still a Garden by the Water blows.

And David's Lips are lock't; but in divine
High-piping Pehlevi, with 'Wine! Wine! Wine!
   '*Red* Wine!' – the Nightingale cries to the Rose
That yellow Cheek of hers to incarnadine.

Come, fill the Cup, and in the Fire of Spring
The Winter Garment of Repentance fling:
   The Bird of Time has but a little way
To fly – and Lo! the Bird is on the Wing.

And look – a thousand Blossoms with the Day
Woke – and a thousand scatter'd into Clay:
   And this first Summer Month that brings the Rose
Shall take Jamshyd and Kaikobad away.

But come with old Khayyam, and leave the Lot
Of Kaikobad and Kaikhosru forgot:
   Let Rustum lay about him as he will,
Or Hatim Tai cry Supper – heed them not.

With me along some Strip of Herbage strown
That just divides the desert from the sown,
   Where name of Slave and Sultan scarce is known,
And pity Sultan Mahmud on his Throne.

Here with a Loaf of Bread beneath the Bough,
A Flask of Wine, a Book of Verse – and Thou
   Beside me singing in the Wilderness –
And Wilderness is Paradise enow.

'How sweet is mortal Sovranty! think some:
Others – 'How blest the Paradise to come!'
   Ah, take the Cash in hand and waive the Rest;
Oh, the brave Music of a *distant* Drum!

JAMES ELROY FLECKER
1884–1915

Herman Elroy Flecker (he later changed his first name to
James) was born on 5 November 1884, the son of the Rev.
W. H. Flecker, headmaster of the City of London School. He
went to Caius College, Cambridge, to study Persian and
Arabic and then joined the diplomatic service. Flecker was
subsequently posted to Constantinople, Smyrna and Beirut,
where he began to suffer from the tuberculosis which was
to kill him. He married in 1911, by which time he had
already published several volumes of verse and had begun
to write for the stage. But two years later his health had
deteriorated to such an extent that he had to enter a
sanitorium in Switzerland, where he completed his play
Hassan. He died on 3 January 1915, and so never lived to
see the enormous success of *Hassan* when staged in
London to music by Delius. Rupert Brooke observed in
his obituary in *The Times* that 'his conversation was varie-
gated, amusing and enriched with booty from the byways of
knowledge'.

92

THE OLD SHIPS

I have seen old ships sail like swans asleep
Beyond the village which men still call Tyre,
With leaden age o'ercargoed, dipping deep
For Famagusta and the hidden sun
That rings black Cyprus with a lake of fire;
And all those ships were certainly so old
Who knows how oft with squat and noisy gun,
Questing brown slaves or Syrian oranges,
The pirates Genoese
Hell-raked them till they rolled
Blood, water, fruit and corpses up the hold.
But now through friendly seas they softly run,
Painted the mid-sea blue or shore-sea green,
Still patterned with the vine and grapes in gold.

But I have seen,
Pointing her shapely shadows from the dawn
And image tumbled on a rose-swept bay,
A drowsy ship of some yet older day;
And, wonder's breath indrawn,
Thought I – who knows – who knows – but in that same
(Fished up beyond Aeaea, patched up new
– Stern painted brighter blue –)
That talkative, bald-headed seaman came
(Twelve patient comrades sweating at the oar)

James Elroy Flecker

From Troy's doom-crimson shore,
And with great lies about his wooden horse
Set the crew laughing, and forgot his course.

It was so old a ship – who knows, who knows?
– And yet so beautiful, I watched in vain
To see the mast burst open with a rose,
And the whole deck put on its leaves again.

ROBERT FROST
1874–1963

━━━ ◦∞∞◦ ━━━

Robert Lee Frost was born in San Francisco on 26 March 1874, of mixed West Country and Scottish stock, and named after the poet Robert Burns and the Confederate General Robert E. Lee. Following the death of his father in 1885, Frost moved with his family to New England where he was educated at Dartmouth College and Harvard. After some experience as a newspaperman, he married in 1895 and inherited a farm from his grandparents.

In 1912 the Frosts came to Britain to run a farm in Buckinghamshire, later moving to Dymock in Gloucestershire. Frost's circle included Ezra Pound, Robert Bridges, Robert Graves and Walter de la Mare as well as the Dymock Poets who included Edward Thomas, Rupert Brooke and Wilfrid Gibson. After his return to America in 1915 he divided his time between writing poetry, teaching and farming, both in New England and in Florida. Eventually he was to win two Pulitzer Prizes, and become America's unofficial Poet Laureate, as well as being praised by President Kennedy and warmly received by Nikita Khrushchev. He died on 29 January 1963, never fulfilling his ambition to win a Nobel Prize.

32

STOPPING BY WOODS
ON A SNOWY EVENING

Whose woods these are I think I know.
His house is in the village though;
He will not see me stopping here
To watch his woods fill up with snow.

My little horse must think it queer
To stop without a farmhouse near
Between the woods and frozen lake
The darkest evening of the year.

He gives his harness bells a shake
To ask if there is some mistake.
The only other sound's the sweep
Of easy wind and downy flake.

The woods are lovely, dark and deep.
But I have promises to keep,
And miles to go before I sleep,
And miles to go before I sleep.

80

THE ROAD NOT TAKEN

Two roads diverged in a yellow wood,
And sorry I could not travel both
And be one traveller, long I stood
And looked down one as far as I could
To where it bent in the undergrowth;

Then took the other, as just as fair,
And having perhaps the better claim,
Because it was grassy and wanted wear;
Though as for that the passing there
Had worn them really about the same,

And both that morning equally lay
In leaves no step had trodden black.
Oh, I kept the first for another day!
Yet knowing how way leads on to way,
I doubted if I should ever come back.

I shall be telling this with a sigh
Somewhere ages and ages hence:
Two roads diverged in a wood, and I –
I took the one less travelled by,
And that has made all the difference.

WILFRID GIBSON
1878–1962

Wilfrid Gibson was born on 2 October 1878 in the North-umberland town of Hexham, the son of a chemist. He was a published poet as early as 1897, but did not move to London until 1912. Here the writer John Middleton Murry was instrumental in introducing him to Edward Marsh and the circle of 'Georgian' poets. Rupert Brooke became a particular friend, and when Gibson and his wife Geraldine moved to the Gloucestershire countryside there was a steady stream of famous visitors including Robert Frost, Edward Thomas and, occasionally, W. H. Davies. Gibson's reputation declined in the 1930s, although he continued to publish poetry until the death of his wife in 1950.

78

THE ICE-CART

Perched on my city office-stool
I watched with envy while a cool
And lucky carter handled ice . . .
And I was wandering in a trice
Far from the grey and grimy heat
Of that intolerable street
O'er sapphire berg and emerald floe
Beneath the still cold ruby glow
Of everlasting Polar night,
Bewildered by the queer half-light,
Until I stumbled unawares
Upon a creek where big white bears
Plunged headlong down with flourished heels
And floundered after shining seals
Through shivering seas of blinding blue.
And, as I watched them, ere I knew
I'd stripped and I was swimming too
Among the seal-pack, young and hale,
And thrusting on with threshing tail,
With twist and twirl and sudden leap
Through crackling ice and salty deep,
Diving and doubling with my kind
Until at last we left behind
Those big white blundering bulks of death,
And lay at length with panting breath

Wilfrid Gibson

Upon a far untravelled floe
Beneath a gentle drift of snow –
Snow drifting gently fine and white
Out of the endless Polar night,
Falling and falling evermore
Upon that far untravelled shore
Till I was buried fathoms deep
Beneath that cold white drifting sleep –
Sleep drifting deep,
Deep drifting sleep . . .

The carter cracked a sudden whip:
I clutched my stool with startled grip,
Awakening to the grimy heat
Of that intolerable street.

THOMAS GRAY
1716–71

---❦---

Gray was born on 26 November 1716, the son of a money-lender. He was educated at Eton and Peterhouse, Cambridge, where he befriended Horace Walpole, one of the sons of Sir Robert Walpole, the first British Prime Minister. The junior Walpole was later to become a famous man of letters himself. Together they toured France and Italy, but quarrelled and returned home separately. Gray went back to Cambridge to take a degree in civil law, but also became one of the first men of learning to take an interest in Norse mythology. When not in his London base near the British Museum, he worked at Peterhouse until the riotous behaviour of the students on his staircase forced him to seek peace and quiet in Pembroke College, where he remained until his death. He frequently visited Stoke Poges in Buckinghamshire where his mother lived and where he was inspired to write many of his elegies. Following the death of Colley Cibber in 1757, Gray was offered the post of Poet Laureate; but he declined with the observation that 'the office itself has always humbled the profession hitherto'. Gray died in Cambridge on 30 July 1771.

16

ELEGY WRITTEN IN A
COUNTRY CHURCHYARD

The curfew tolls the Knell of parting Day,
The lowing Herd winds slowly o'er the Lea,
The Plow-man homeward plods his weary Way,
And leaves the World to Darkness, and to me.

Now fades the glimmering Landscape on the Sight,
And all the Air a solemn Stillness holds;
Save where the Beetle wheels his droning Flight,
And drowsy Tinklings lull the distant Folds.

Save that from yonder Ivy-mantled Tow'r
The mopeing Owl does to the Moon complain
Of such as, wand'ring near her secret Bow'r,
Molest her ancient solitary Reign.

Beneath whose rugged Elms, that Yew-Tree's Shade,
Where heaves the Turf in many a mould'ring Heap,
Each in his narrow Cell for ever laid,
The rude Forefathers of the Hamlet sleep.

The breezy Call of Incense-breathing Morn,
The Swallow twitt'ring from the Straw-built Shed,
The Cock's shrill Clarion, or the echoing Horn,
No more shall rouse them from their lowly Bed.

For them no more the blazing Hearth shall burn,
Or busy Houswife ply her Evening Care:
No Children run to lisp their Sire's Return,
Or climb his Knees the envied Kiss to share.

Oft did the Harvest to their Sickle yield,
Their Furrow oft the stubborn Glebe has broke;
How jocund did they drive their Team afield!
How bow'd the Woods beneath their sturdy Stroke!
Let not Ambition mock their useful Toil,
Their homely Joys and Destiny obscure;
Nor Grandeur hear with a disdainful Smile,
The short and simple Annals of the Poor.
The Boast of Heraldry, the Pomp of Pow'r,
And all that Beauty, all that Wealth e'er gave,
Awaits alike th'inevitable Hour.
The Paths of Glory lead but to the Grave.

Nor you, ye Proud, impute to these the Fault,
If Mem'ry o'er their Tomb no Trophies raise,
Where thro' the long-drawn Isle and fretted Vault
The pealing Anthem swells the Note of Praise.
Can storied Urn or animated Bust
Back to its Mansion call the fleeting Breath?
Can Honour's Voice provoke the silent Dust,
Or Flatt'ry sooth the dull cold Ear of Death?

Perhaps in this neglected Spot is laid
Some Heart once pregnant with celestial Fire,
Hands that the Rod of Empire might have sway'd,
Or wak'd to Extacy the living Lyre.
But Knowledge to their Eyes her ample Page
Rich with the Spoils of Time did ne'er unroll;
Chill Penury repress'd their noble Rage,
And froze the genial Current of the Soul.
Full many a Gem of purest Ray serene,
The dark unfathom'd Caves of Ocean bear:

Thomas Gray

Full many a Flower is born to blush unseen,
And waste its Sweetness on the desert Air.
    Some Village-*Hampden* that with dauntless Breast
The little Tyrant of his Fields withstood;
Some mute inglorious *Milton* here may rest,
Some *Cromwell* guiltless of his Country's Blood.

    Th'Applause of list'ning Senates to command,
The Threats of Pain and Ruin to despise,
To scatter Plenty o'er a smiling Land,
And read their Hist'ry in a Nation's Eyes

    Their Lot forbad: nor circumscrib'd alone
Their growing Virtues, but their Crimes confin'd;
Forbad to wade through Slaughter to a Throne,
And shut the Gates of Mercy on Mankind,

    The struggling Pangs of conscious Truth to hide,
To quench the Blushes of ingenuous Shame,
Or heap the Shrine of Luxury and Pride
With Incense, kindled at the Muse's Flame.

    Far from the madding Crowd's ignoble Strife,
Their sober Wishes never learn'd to stray;
Along the cool sequester'd Vale of Life
They kept the noiseless Tenor of their Way.

    Yet ev'n these Bones from Insult to protect
Some frail Memorial still erected nigh,
With uncouth Rhimes and shapeless Sculpture deck'd,
Implores the passing Tribute of a Sigh.

    Their Name, their Years, spelt by th'unletter'd Muse,
The Place of Fame and Elegy supply:
And many a holy Text around she strews,
That teach the rustic Moralist to dye.

For who to dumb Forgetfulness a Prey,
This pleasing anxious Being e'er resign'd,
Left the warm Precincts of the cheerful Day,
Nor cast one longing ling'ring Look behind?

On some fond Breast the parting Soul relies,
Some pious Drops the closing Eye requires;
Ev'n from the Tomb the Voice of Nature cries,
Ev'n in our Ashes live their wonted Fires.

For thee, who mindful of th'unhonour'd Dead
Dost in these Lines their artless Tale relate;
If chance, by lonely Contemplation led,
Some kindred Spirit shall inquire thy Fate,

Haply some hoary-headed Swain may say,
'Oft have we seen him at the Peep of Dawn
'Brushing with hasty Steps the Dews away
'To meet the Sun upon the upland Lawn.

'There at the Foot of yonder nodding Beech
'That wreathes its old fantastic Roots so high,
'His listless Length at Noontide wou'd he stretch,
'And pore upon the Brook that babbles by.

'Hard by yon Wood, now smiling as in Scorn,
'Mutt'ring his wayward Fancies he wou'd rove,
'Now drooping, woeful wan, like one forlorn,
'Or craz'd with Care, or cross'd in hopeless Love.

'One Morn I miss'd him on the custom'd Hill,
'Along the Heath, and near his fav'rite Tree;
'Another came; nor yet beside the Rill,
'Nor up the Lawn, nor at the Wood was he.

'The next with Dirges due in sad Array
'Slow thro' the Church-way Path we saw him born.

Thomas Gray

'Approach and read (for thou can'st read) the Lay,
'Grav'd on the Stone beneath yon aged Thorn.'
   (There scatter'd oft, the earliest of the Year,
By Hands unseen, are Show'rs of Violets found:
The Red-breast loves to bill and warble there,
And little Footsteps lightly print the Ground.)

THE EPITAPH

*Here rests his Head upon the Lap of Earth
A Youth to Fortune and to Fame unknown:
Fair Science frown'd not on his humble Birth,
And Melancholy mark'd him for her own.
   Large was his Bounty, and his Soul sincere,
Heav'n did a Recompence as largely send:
He gave to Mis'ry all he had, a Tear:
He gain'd from Heav'n ('twas all he wish'd) a Friend.
   No farther seek his Merits to disclose,
Or draw his Frailties from their dread Abode,
(There they alike in trembling Hope repose)
The Bosom of his Father and his God.*

THOMAS HARDY
1840–1928

Hardy was born on 2 June 1840 in Higher Bockhampton near Dorchester, the son of a builder and of a mother who worked in domestic service. While his father, a gifted musician, taught Hardy to play the violin, he was encouraged by his mother to pursue his literary ambitions. He left school in Dorchester at the age of sixteen to become apprenticed to a London architect and in 1868, while on an architectural mission to Cornwall, met Emma Gifford. Six years later, a successful novelist, he could afford to abandon architecture and marry Emma. For three years from 1878 the Hardys lived in Tooting in London, mixing with literary notables including Browning, Tennyson, Henry James and Matthew Arnold.

In 1887 the Hardys returned to the countryside – to the house that he had designed near Dorchester. After the critical drubbing he received for *Tess of the D'Urbervilles* (1891) and *Jude the Obscure* (1895) Hardy returned to poetry, his first love. In 1912 Emma died and about the same time Hardy found himself restored to favour. He was awarded honorary degrees from both Oxford and Cambridge, was made a Fellow of the Royal Society of Literature and given the Order of Merit. When he died, on 11 January 1928, his heart was buried with his parents and Emma at

Stinsford in Dorset, while his other remains rest in Westminster Abbey – a decision taken by his second wife, Florence.

67

WEATHERS

This is the weather the cuckoo likes,
　　And so do I;
When showers betumble the chestnut spikes,
　　And nestlings fly:
And the little brown nightingale bills his best,
And they sit outside at 'The Travellers' Rest',
And maids come forth sprig-muslin drest,
And citizens dream of the south and west,
　　And so do I.

This is the weather the shepherd shuns,
　　And so do I;
When beeches drip in brown and duns,
　　And thresh, and ply;
And hill-hid tides throb, throe on throe,
And meadow rivulets overflow,
And drops on gate-bars hang in a row,
And rooks in families homeward go,
　　And so do I.

W. E. HENLEY
1849–1903

William Ernest Henley was born in Gloucester on 23 August
1849, the son of a bookseller. An attack of tubercular
arthritis during childhood resulted in the amputation of
his left foot and part of the left leg, and only a spell in
Edinburgh's Royal Infirmary and the skills of the great
surgeon Sir Joseph Lister saved the right leg. While in
hospital he became a close friend of Robert Louis Stevenson, with whom he collaborated on four plays, notably
Deacon Brodie. Stevenson described his friend as 'boister-
ous and piratical', and Henley's deformity and character
made him an obvious model for Long John Silver in
Stevenson's *Treasure Island*. As editor of a succession
of influential publications Henley was able to publish
the work of Hardy, Kipling, Yeats, Henry James and
H. G. Wells, and he was a devoted champion of the painter
Whistler. Like many of his contemporaries, Henley was a
man of patriotic if not downright jingoistic views. Four
years after his death, on 11 June 1903, Rodin's monument
to Henley was formally handed over to the Chapter of
St Paul's Cathedral. In his address, Henley's friend George
Wyndham referred to both the work and the man as
'monumental without being sepulchral'.

INVICTUS

IV
I. M.
R. T. Hamilton Bruce
(1846–1899)

Out of the night that covers me,
  Black as the Pit from pole to pole,
I thank whatever gods may be
  For my unconquerable soul.

In the fell clutch of circumstance
  I have not winced nor cried aloud.
Under the bludgeonings of chance
  My head is bloody, but unbowed.

Beyond this place of wrath and tears
  Looms but the Horror of the shade,
And yet the menace of the years
  Finds, and shall find, me unafraid.

It matters not how strait the gate,
  How charged with punishments the scroll,
I am the master of my fate:
  I am the captain of my soul.

ROBERT HERRICK
1591–1674

⸻ ∞ ⸻

Herrick was born in London in August 1591, the seventh child of a Leicester goldsmith. He followed the family business, becoming apprenticed to his uncle, until 1613 when he entered St John's College, Cambridge. Four years later he moved to Trinity Hall where he took his degree. After taking holy orders Herrick became army chaplain on the Duke of Buckingham's expedition to aid the Protestant forces besieged at La Rochelle, and he was rewarded with the living at Dean Prior in Devon where he wrote many of his poems. For a while he left Dean Prior in order to take up residence in London with a woman many years his junior with whom he allegedly had a daughter. During Cromwell's Protectorate he suffered for his Royalist connections, only regaining his former position with the Restoration of Charles II in 1660. He returned to Dean Prior but wrote no more poetry, dying in October 1674.

77

TO DAFFODILS

Fair Daffodils, we weep to see
    You haste away so soon;
As yet the early rising sun
    Has not attained his noon.
        Stay, stay,
    Until the hasting day
        Has run
    But to the evensong,
And, having prayed together, we
    Will go with you along.

We have short time to stay, as you,
    We have as short a spring;
As quick a growth to meet decay,
    As you, or any thing.
        We die,
    As your hours do, and dry
        Away,
    Like to the summer's rain;
Or as the pearls of morning's dew,
    Ne'er to be found again.

RALPH HODGSON
1871–1962

———— ୧∞৪০ ————

Ralph Edwin Hodgson was born in Darlington on 9 September 1871, the son of a coal-miner. A champion boxer and billiards player, he worked in the theatre in New York before returning to London to work as a draughtsman on several evening newspapers. With Lovat Fraser he set up a publishing house; then, after editing *Fry's Magazine,* he took a post as Lecturer in English Studies at Tohuku University in Japan in early 1924. His friend and fellow poet Edmund Blunden also took up a teaching post in Japan several months later. Outside his academic work he judged the Bull Terrier class at Crufts Dog Show. In 1938 he retired from teaching and settled in Ohio, resuming his work as a poet. He was one of the earliest writers to be concerned with ecology, speaking out against the fur trade and man's destruction of the natural world. He died on 3 November 1962.

85

THE BELLS OF HEAVEN

'Twould ring the bells of Heaven
The wildest peal for years,
If Parson lost his senses
And people came to theirs,
And he and they together
Knelt down with angry prayers
For tamed and shabby tigers
And dancing dogs and bears,
And wretched, blind pit ponies,
And little hunted hares.

THOMAS HOOD
1799–1845

Hood was born in London on 23 May 1799, the son of a bookseller. Sent to Dundee to convalesce after tuberculosis, he began to contribute to local newspapers and periodicals before returning to London to continue his career in journalism. Assistant editor of the *London Magazine* at only twenty-two, he moved in literary circles where he met Hazlitt, Charles Lamb and Thomas de Quincey. He quickly became famous for his satirical wit, which he put to good use in his editorship of *The Gem* and its comic annual. One of his admirers described him as 'the starry soul, that shines when all is dark!', and he was of sufficient reputation to be a serious contender for the post of Poet Laureate after Southey's death in 1843. Shortly before his own death on 3 May 1845 he published his poem 'The Bridge of Sighs', which Thackeray described as 'his Corunna, his Heights of Abraham' – a great victory achieved in his dying hour. Another of his achievements was 'The Song of the Shirt', written anonymously for *Punch* in protest against the awful conditions in which the mass of the population had to work.

28

I REMEMBER, I REMEMBER

I remember, I remember,
   The house where I was born,
The little window where the sun
   Came peeping in at morn;
He never came a wink too soon,
   Nor brought too long a day,
But now, I often wish the night
   Had borne my breath away.

I remember, I remember,
   The roses, red and white;
The violets, and the lily-cups,
   Those flowers made of light!
The lilacs where the robin built,
   And where my brother set
The laburnum on his birthday –
   The tree is living yet!

I remember, I remember,
   Where I was used to swing;
And thought the air must rush as fresh
   To swallows on the wing:
My spirit flew in feathers then,
   That is so heavy now,
And summer pools could hardly cool
   The fever on my brow!

Thomas Hood

I remember, I remember,
    The fir trees dark and high;
I used to think their slender tops
    Were close against the sky:
It was a childish ignorance,
    But now 'tis little joy
To know I'm farther off from Heav'n
    Than when I was a boy.

GERARD MANLEY HOPKINS
1844–89

———— ❦ ————

Hopkins was born in Stratford, Essex, in 1844, the eldest son of a prosperous and artistically inclined family. His father had published a collection of poems dedicated to Thomas Hood, while two of Hopkins' brothers became professional artists. After attending Highgate School in London, he went up to Balliol College, Oxford, to read classics and began a lifelong friendship with the poet Robert Bridges. Influenced by the ideas of Newman, founder of the High Church Oxford Movement, Hopkins became a Catholic, entering the Jesuit Order in 1868 and burning all his existing poems. Fortunately, Bridges retained copies which he kept in safety; very little of Hopkins' poetry was published during his life, but after his death Bridges brought his work to prominence.

Hopkins' physical and mental state was never strong; only while on holiday from his various teaching posts could he devote himself to his poetry, developing his use of what he called the 'sprung rhythm'. He sank increasingly into depression at what he perceived to be his faults and failings, and his health declined still further after he was appointed to the Chair of Classics at University College, Dublin. He fell easy prey to an outbreak of typhoid in the Irish capital in June 1889. He is buried in Dublin, but in the transept of Westminster Abbey there is a memorial stone to Hopkins in the company of his fellow poets Tennyson, Masefield, Browning, Eliot and Auden.

42

PIED BEAUTY

Glory be to God for dappled things –
  For skies of couple-colour as a brinded cow;
    For rose-moles all in stipple upon trout that swim;
Fresh-firecoal chestnut-falls; finches' wings;
  Landscape plotted and pieced – fold, fallow, and plough;
    And all trades, their gear and tackle and trim.

All things counter, original, spare, strange;
  Whatever is fickle, freckled (who knows how?)
    With swift, slow; sweet, sour; adazzle, dim;
He fathers-forth whose beauty is past change:
                Praise him.

63

THE WINDHOVER

To Christ our Lord

I caught this morning morning's minion kingdom, of
    daylight's dauphin, dapple-dawn-drawn Falcon, in his
    riding
  Of the rolling level underneath him steady air, and
    striding
High there, how he rung upon the rein of a wimpling wing
In his ecstasy! then off, off forth on swing,
  As a skate's heel sweeps smooth on a bow-bend: the hurl
    and gliding
  Rebuffed the big wind. My heart in hiding
Stirred for a bird, – the achieve of, the mastery of the thing!

Brute beauty and valour and act, oh, air, pride, plume, here
  Buckle! AND the fire that breaks from thee then, a billion
Times told lovelier, more dangerous, O my chevalier!

  No wonder of it: sheer plod makes plough down sillion
Shine, and blue-bleak embers, ah my dear,
  Fall, gall themselves, and gash gold-vermilion.

A. E. HOUSMAN
1859–1936

——— ∞∞∞ ———

Alfred Edward Housman was born on 26 March 1859, the eldest of the seven children of a solicitor in Bromsgrove, Worcestershire. From the local high school he went on to St John's College, Oxford, where, despite his brilliance as a scholar, he failed his Finals. It is thought that the reason for his poor performance was his deep passion for his fellow student Moses Jackson, which would remain with him for the rest of his life. Jackson's decision to emigrate to India and his subsequent marriage there produced an outpouring of emotion which Housman expressed through his poetry.

When Housman was not working as a clerk at the London Patent Office, he would be in the British Museum reading the classics with such dedication that eventually he became Professor of Classics at University College, London. His collection *A Shropshire Lad*, from which 'Loveliest of Trees, the Cherry Now' is taken, found extraordinary favour with the public, selling up to fifteen thousand copies a year during the First World War. Housman's work was also set to music by composers such as Vaughan Williams, Butterworth and Ireland. The news of Jackson's impending death in the 1920s led to a further burst of poetic creativity. Appointed Professor of Latin at Trinity College, Cambridge, in 1911, Housman remained at Cambridge until his death on 30 April 1936.

A. E. Housman

12

LOVELIEST OF TREES, THE CHERRY NOW

Loveliest of trees, the cherry now
Is hung with bloom along the bough,
And stands about the woodland ride
Wearing white for Eastertide.

Now, of my threescore years and ten,
Twenty will not come again,
And take from seventy springs a score,
It only leaves me fifty more.

And since to look at things in bloom
Fifty springs are little room,
About the woodlands I will go
To see the cherry hung with snow.

LEIGH HUNT
1784–1859

James Henry Leigh Hunt was born at Eagle Hall, Southgate, Middlesex, on 19 October 1784, the son of an American lawyer turned clergyman and the grandson of a Philadelphia merchant. At the age of seven he was admitted as a charity pupil at Christ's Hospital grammar school, and then spent some time in a lawyer's office before becoming a journalist. With his older brother John he founded the *Examiner*, but fell foul of the libel laws when he incautiously added the words 'at fifty' to a tribute in the paper which described the Prince Regent as 'an Adonis'. For the two years of his prison sentence Leigh Hunt continued to edit the *Examiner* and to entertain friends such as Charles Lamb and Byron, who considered that Leigh Hunt had 'a great independence of spirit'. The place where the gaol once stood in Southwark is now known as Leigh Hunt Street. Such is infamy!

Once released from prison, Leigh Hunt, with his growing family, led a peripatetic existence around London, their typical home described thus: 'over the dusty table and ragged carpet lie all kinds of litter – books, paper, eggshells, scissors and . . . the torn heart of a half-quarter loaf'. Despite such domestic chaos, Leigh Hunt found time to publish the work of Keats and to befriend Wordsworth, Thomas Hood, Shelley and Carlyle. He spent his last years in Kensington, dying on 28 August 1859. 'Abou Ben Adhem' was first published in an anthology of 1838 and has remained popular ever since.

34

ABOU BEN ADHEM

Abou Ben Adhem (may his tribe increase!)
Awoke one night from a deep dream of peace,
And saw, within the moonlight in his room,
Making it rich, and like a lily in bloom,
An angel writing in a book of gold: –
Exceeding peace had made Ben Adhem bold,
And to the presence in the room he said,
  'What writest thou?' – The vision raised its head,
And with a look made of all sweet accord,
Answered, 'The names of those who love the Lord.'
'And is mine one?' said Abou. 'Nay, not so,'
Replied the angel. Abou spoke more low,
But cheerly still; and said, 'I pray thee, then,
Write me as one that loves his fellow-men.'
  The angel wrote, and vanished. The next night
It came again with a great wakening light,
And showed the names whom love of God had blest,
And lo! Ben Adhem's name led all the rest.

JENNY JOSEPH
born 1932

———— ∞∞∞ ————

Jenefer Ruth Joseph was born in Birmingham on 7 May 1932 and read English at St Hilda's College, Oxford. She then worked as a reporter before moving to South Africa for two years. Her first collection of poems was published in 1960 but she still had to make a living, running a London pub from 1969 to 1972 and then teaching and lecturing in extra-mural and adult education. She has continued to write award-winning verse through the subsequent decades, as well as turning to fiction for which she received the James Tait Black Memorial Award in 1986. Commenting on her own work, she has observed that 'It is usually easier for a writer to talk about what he or she is doing "now" or "next" than about what has been done.' Jenny Joseph is the only living poet in the Classic FM Top 100.

43

WARNING

When I am an old woman I shall wear purple
With a red hat which doesn't go, and doesn't suit me,
And I shall spend my pension on brandy and summer
    gloves
And satin sandals, and say we've no money for butter.
I shall sit down on the pavement when I'm tired
And gobble up samples in shops and press alarm bells
And run my stick along the public railings
And make up for the sobriety of my youth.
I shall go out in my slippers in the rain
And pick the flowers in other people's gardens
And learn to spit.

You can wear terrible shirts and grow more fat
And eat three pounds of sausages at a go
Or only bread and pickle for a week
And hoard pens and pencils and beermats and things in
    boxes.

But now we must have clothes that keep us dry
And pay our rent and not swear in the street
And set a good example for the children.
We must have friends to dinner and read the papers.

Jenny Joseph

But maybe I ought to practise a little now?
So people who know me are not too shocked and
    surprised
When suddenly I am old, and start to wear purple.

JOHN KEATS
1796–1821

———◦∞◦———

Keats was born on 29 October 1796 in North London, the grandson of the proprietor of a livery stables. After receiving a basic classical education at an Enfield school he became apprenticed to a surgeon in nearby Edmonton, but his friendship with the son of his teacher encouraged his writing of poetry and led to his meeting Leigh Hunt. Keats and Leigh Hunt took countless walks around Hampstead Heath and Highgate, areas which were to inspire many of Keats' works. After studying at Guy's Hospital and qualifying as a surgeon/apothecary Keats concentrated on writing poetry, but the lukewarm response of the press adversely affected his already enfeebled physical and mental state. He travelled through Scotland, Devon and the Isle of Wight, producing poetry which was nevertheless warmly received by his fellow writers. He became engaged to his Hampstead neighbour Fanny Brawne, and in a vain attempt to escape the advance of the consumption that was to kill him accepted Shelley's invitation to go to Italy. On 27 December 1821 Keats died in Rome at the age of just twenty-four and was buried in the English Cemetery there. Shelley, the chief mourner, was soon to join him.

7

TO AUTUMN

Season of mists and mellow fruitfulness,
   Close bosom-friend of the maturing sun;
Conspiring with him how to load and bless
   With fruit the vines that round the thatch-eaves run;
To bend with apples the moss'd cottage-trees,
   And fill all fruit with ripeness to the core;
     To swell the gourd, and plump the hazel shells
With a sweet kernel; to set budding more,
   And still more, later flowers for the bees,
   Until they think warm days will never cease,
   For Summer has o'er-brimm'd their clammy cells.

Who hath not seen thee oft amid thy store?
   Sometimes whoever seeks abroad may find
Thee sitting careless on a granary floor,
   Thy hair soft-lifted by the winnowing wind;
Or on a half-reap'd furrow sound asleep,
   Drows'd with the fume of poppies, while thy hook
     Spares the next swath and all its twined flowers:
And sometimes like a gleaner thou dost keep
   Steady thy laden head across a brook;
   Or by a cider-press, with patient look,
   Thou watchest the last oozings, hours by hours.

Where are the songs of Spring? Ay, where are they?
   Think not of them, thou hast thy music too, –
While barred clouds bloom the soft-dying day,
   And touch the stubble-plains with rosy hue;
Then in a wailful choir the small gnats mourn
   Among the river sallows, borne aloft
     Or sinking as the light wind lives or dies;
And full-grown lambs loud bleat from hilly bourn;
   Hedge-crickets sing; and now with treble soft
The red-breast whistles from a garden croft;
     And gathering swallows twitter in the skies.

John Keats

24

ODE TO A NIGHTINGALE

My heart aches, and a drowsy numbness pains
   My sense, as though of hemlock I had drunk,
Or emptied some dull opiate to the drains
   One minute past, and Lethe-wards had sunk:
'Tis not through envy of thy happy lot,
   But being too happy in thy happiness, –
      That thou, light-winged Dryad of the trees,
         In some melodious plot
Of beechen green, and shadows numberless,
     Singest of summer in full-throated ease.

O for a draught of vintage! that hath been
   Cool'd a long age in the deep-delved earth,
Tasting of Flora and the country-green,
   Dance, and Provençal song, and sunburnt mirth!
O for a beaker full of the warm South,
   Full of the true, the blushful Hippocrene,
      With beaded bubbles winking at the brim,
         And purple-stained mouth;
That I might drink, and leave the world unseen,
   And with thee fade away into the forest dim:

Fade far away, dissolve, and quite forget
   What thou among the leaves hast never known,
The weariness, the fever, and the fret
   Here, where men sit and hear each other groan;
Where palsy shakes a few, sad, last grey hairs,
     Where youth grows pale, and spectre-thin, and dies;
        Where but to think is to be full of sorrow
            And leaden-eyed despairs;
     Where Beauty cannot keep her lustrous eyes,
     Or new Love pine at them beyond tomorrow.

Away! away! for I will fly to thee,
   Not charioted by Bacchus and his pards,
But on the viewless wings of Poesy,
   Though the dull brain perplexes and retards:
Already with thee! tender is the night,
     And haply the Queen-Moon is on her throne,
        Cluster'd around by all her starry Fays;
            But here there is no light,
Save what from heaven is with the breezes blown
   Through verdurous glooms and winding mossy ways.

.I cannot see what flowers are at my feet,
   Nor what soft incense hangs upon the boughs,
But, in embalmed darkness, guess each sweet
   Wherewith the seasonable month endows
The grass, the thicket, and the fruit-tree wild;
     White hawthorn, and the pastoral eglantine;
        Fast-fading violets cover'd up in leaves;
           And mid-May's eldest child,
   The coming musk-rose, full of dewy wine,
     The murmurous haunt of flies on summer eves.

Darkling I listen; and for many a time
  I have been half in love with easeful Death,
Call'd him soft names in many a musèd rhyme,
  To take into the air my quiet breath;
Now more than ever seems it rich to die,
  To cease upon the midnight with no pain,
    While thou art pouring forth thy soul abroad
      In such an ecstasy!
  Still wouldst thou sing, and I have ears in vain –
    To thy high requiem become a sod.

Thou wast not born for death, immortal Bird!
  No hungry generations tread thee down;
The voice I hear this passing night was heard
  In ancient days by emperor and clown:
Perhaps the self-same song that found a path
  Through the sad heart of Ruth, when, sick for home,
    She stood in tears amid the alien corn;
      The same that oft-times hath
  Charm'd magic casements, opening on the foam
    Of perilous seas, in faery lands forlorn.

Forlorn! the very word is like a bell
  To toll me back from thee to my sole self!
Adieu! the fancy cannot cheat so well
  As she is fam'd to do, deceiving elf.
Adieu! adieu! thy plaintive anthem fades
  Past the near meadows, over the still stream,
    Up the hill-side; and now 'tis buried deep
      In the next valley-glades:
  Was it a vision, or a waking dream?
    Fled is that music: – Do I wake or sleep?

41

ODE ON A GRECIAN URN

Thou still unravish'd bride of quietness,
  Thou foster-child of silence and slow time,
Sylvan historian, who canst thus express
  A flowery tale more sweetly than our rhyme:
What leaf-fring'd legend haunts about thy shape
  Of deities or mortals, or of both,
    In Tempe or the dales of Arcady?
What men or gods are these? What maidens loath?
  What mad pursuit? What struggle to escape?
    What pipes and timbrels? What wild ecstasy?

Heard melodies are sweet, but those unheard
  Are sweeter; therefore, ye soft pipes, play on;
Not to the sensual ear, but, more endear'd,
  Pipe to the spirit ditties of no tone:
Fair youth beneath the trees, thou canst not leave
  Thy song, nor ever can those trees be bare;
    Bold Lover, never, never canst thou kiss,
Though winning near the goal – yet, do not grieve;
  She cannot fade, though thou hast not thy bliss,
    For ever wilt thou love, and she be fair!

  Ah, happy, happy boughs! that cannot shed
    Your leaves, nor ever bid the Spring adieu;

And, happy melodist, unwearied,
  For ever piping songs for ever new;
More happy love! more happy, happy love!
  For ever warm and still to be enjoy'd,
    For ever panting, and for ever young;
All breathing human passions far above,
  That leaves a heart high-sorrowful and cloy'd,
    A burning forehead, and a parching tongue.

Who are these coming to the sacrifice?
  To what green altar, O mysterious priest,
Lead'st thou that heifer lowing at the skies,
  And all her silken flanks with garlands drest?
What little town by river or sea shore,
  Or mountain-built with peaceful citadel,
    Is emptied of its folk, this pious morn?
And, little town, thy streets for evermore
  Will silent be; and not a soul to tell
    Why thou art desolate, can e'er return.

O Attic shape! Fair attitude! with brede
  Of marble men and maidens overwrought,
With forest branches and the trodden weed;
  Thou, silent form, dost tease us out of thought
As doth eternity: Cold Pastoral!
  When old age shall this generation waste,
    Thou shalt remain, in midst of other woe
Than ours, a friend to man, to whom thou say'st,
  'Beauty is truth, truth beauty,' – that is all
    Ye know on earth, and all ye need to know.

70

LA BELLE DAME SANS MERCI

'O what can ail thee, knight-at-arms,
   Alone and palely loitering?
The sedge has wither'd from the lake,
      And no birds sing.

'O what can ail thee, knight-at-arms!
      So haggard and so woe-begone?
The squirrel's granary is full,
   And the harvest's done.

'I see a lily on thy brow
   With anguish moist and fever-dew,
And on thy cheeks a fading rose
   Fast withereth too.'

'I met a lady in the meads,
   Full beautiful – a faery's child,
Her hair was long, her foot was light,
   And her eyes were wild.

'I made a garland for her head,
   And bracelets too, and fragrant zone;
She look'd at me as she did love,
   And made sweet moan.

'I set her on my pacing steed
    And nothing else saw all day long,
For sidelong would she bend, and sing
    A faery's song.

'She found me roots of relish sweet,
    And honey wild and manna-dew,
And sure in language strange she said
        "I love thee true."

'She took me to her elfin grot,
    And there she wept, and sigh'd full sore,
And there I shut her wild wild eyes
    With kisses four.

'And there she lulled me asleep
    And there I dream'd – Ah! Woe betide!
The latest dream I ever dream'd
    On the cold hill side.

'I saw pale kings and princes too,
    Pale warriors, death-pale were they all;
They cried – "La Belle Dame sans Merci
        Hath thee in thrall!"

'I saw their starv'd lips in the gloam
    With horrid warning gapèd wide,
And I awoke and found me here
    On the cold hill's side.

'And this is why I sojourn here
    Alone and palely loitering,
Though the sedge is wither'd from the lake
    And no birds sing.'

RUDYARD KIPLING
1865–1936

———— ∞∞∞ ————

Kipling was born on 30 December 1865 in Bombay, India; his artist/sculptor father and writer/poet mother who had first met on the shores of Lake Rudyard in Staffordshire. Among his close relatives were the painter Burne-Jones and the future Prime Minister Stanley Baldwin. At the age of six Kipling was despatched to England to the care of a Southsea woman who treated him with great cruelty. He was then sent to be educated at the United Services College at Westward Ho! in North Devon, where the short-sighted boy was dubbed 'gig-lamps' by his fellow pupils. However, his obvious literary talents were recognised by the headmaster, who appointed him editor of the school magazine.

At the age of sixteen Kipling rejoined his parents in Lahore, where he found work on the local newspaper and gained all-round journalistic experience. He left for England in 1889, marrying three years later. However, two of the three children of the marriage were to die before their parents, including his adored son John at the Battle of Loos in the First World War. Kipling himself died on 18 January 1936 at Batemans, his house in East Sussex.

Walt Disney's animated film of Kipling's children's classic *The Jungle Book* brought global recognition for book and author.

2

IF
('Brother Square-Toes' – *Rewards and Fairies*)

If you can keep your head when all about you
    Are losing theirs and blaming it on you,
If you can trust yourself when all men doubt you,
    But make allowance for their doubting too;
If you can wait and not be tired by waiting,
    Or being lied about, don't deal in lies,
Or being hated, don't give way to hating,
    And yet don't look too good, nor talk too wise:

If you can dream – and not make dreams your master;
    If you can think – and not make thoughts your aim;
If you can meet with Triumph and Disaster
    And treat those two impostors just the same;
If you can bear to hear the truth you've spoken
    Twisted by knaves to make a trap for fools,
Or watch the things you gave your life to, broken,
    And stoop and build 'em up with worn-out tools:

If you can make one heap of all your winnings
    And risk it on one turn of pitch-and-toss,
And lose, and start again at your beginnings
    And never breathe a word about your loss;

If you can force your heart and nerve and sinew
   To serve your turn long after they are gone,
And so hold on when there is nothing in you
   Except the Will which says to them: 'Hold on!'

If you can talk with crowds and keep your virtue,
   Or walk with Kings – nor lose the common touch,
If neither foes nor loving friends can hurt you,
   If all men count with you, but none too much;
If you can fill the unforgiving minute
   With sixty seconds' worth of distance run,
Yours is the Earth and everything that's in it,
   And – which is more – you'll be a Man, my son!

29

THE WAY THROUGH THE WOODS

('Marklake Witches' – *Rewards and Fairies*)

They shut the road through the woods
Seventy years ago.
Weather and rain have undone it again,
And now you would never know
There was once a road through the woods
Before they planted the trees.
It is underneath the coppice and heath
And the thin anemones.
Only the keeper sees
That, where the ring-dove broods,
And the badgers roll at ease,
There was once a road through the woods.

Yet, if you enter the woods
Of a summer evening late,
When the night-air cools on the trout-ringed pools
Where the otter whistles his mate,
(They fear not men in the woods,
Because they see so few.)
You will hear the beat of a horse's feet,
And the swish of a skirt in the dew,
Steadily cantering through
The misty solitudes,

Rudyard Kipling

As though they perfectly knew
The old lost road through the woods . . .
But there is no road through the woods.

61

THE GLORY OF THE GARDEN

Our England is a garden that is full of stately views,
Of borders, beds and shrubberies and lawns and avenues,
With statues on the terraces and peacocks strutting by;
But the Glory of the Garden lies in more than meets the eye.

For where the old thick laurels grow, along the thin red
    wall,
You find the tool- and potting-sheds which are the heart of
    all;
The cold-frames and the hot-houses, the dungpits and the
    tanks,
The rollers, carts and drain-pipes, with the barrows and the
    planks.

And there you'll see the gardeners, the men and 'prentice
    boys
Told off to do as they are bid and do it without noise;
For, except when seeds are planted and we shout to scare
    the birds,
The Glory of the Garden it abideth not in words.

And some can pot begonias and some can bud a rose,
And some are hardly fit to trust with anything that grows;

But they can roll and trim the lawns and sift the sand and
   loam,
For the Glory of the Garden occupieth all who come.

Our England is a garden, and such gardens are not made
By singing:– 'Oh, how beautiful!' and sitting in the shade,
While better men than we go out and start their working
   lives
At grubbing weeds from gravel-paths with broken
   dinner-knives.

There's not a pair of legs so thin, there's not a head so thick,
There's not a hand so weak and white, nor yet a heart so
   sick,
But it can find some needful job that's crying to be done,
For the Glory of the Garden glorifieth every one.

Then seek your job with thankfulness and work till
   further orders,
If it's only netting strawberries or killing slugs on borders;
And when your back stops aching and your hands begin
   to harden,
You will find yourself a partner in the Glory of the Garden.

Oh, Adam was a gardener, and God who made him sees
That half a proper gardener's work is done upon his knees,
So when your work is finished, you can wash your hands
   and pray
For the Glory of the Garden, that it may not pass away!
And the Glory of the Garden it shall never pass away!

PHILIP LARKIN
1922–85

Philip Larkin was born in Coventry on 9 August 1922, the son of the City Treasurer. He attended the King Henry VIII School before going up to St John's College, Cambridge, where he met Kingsley Amis, the future novelist and poet who became his close friend. After university he became a librarian, first at Leicester University, then in Belfast, and finally in Hull, where he moved in 1955 and where he was to remain until the end of his life. He published his first volume of poetry in 1945 and ten years later had become a poet of some standing, often being included with Kingsley Amis and John Wain as writers whose love of poetry was mingled with a love of jazz.

Larkin never married, but shared his life in Hull from 1974 with Monica Jones. Latterly, frustrated by increasing deafness, he wrote little poetry. On the death of his friend John Betjeman in 1984 he was invited to become Poet Laureate but, despite his admiration for the Prime Minister, Margaret Thatcher, he declined. Within a year Larkin followed Betjeman to the grave. Although his will specifically stated that all his papers should be burned, his instructions were contradictory and so were not carried out.

60

THE WHITSUN WEDDINGS

That Whitsun, I was late getting away:
  Not till about
One-twenty on the sunlit Saturday
Did my three-quarters-empty train pull out,
All windows down, all cushions hot, all sense
Of being in a hurry gone. We ran
Behind the backs of houses, crossed a street
Of blinding windscreens, smelt the fish-dock, thence
The river's level drifting breadth began,
Where sky and Lincolnshire and water meet.

All afternoon, through the tall heat that slept
  For miles inland,
A slow and stopping curve southwards we kept.
Wide farms went by, short-shadowed cattle, and
Canals with floatings of industrial froth;
A hothouse flashed uniquely: hedges dipped
And rose: and now and then a smell of grass
Displaced the reek of buttoned carriage-cloth
Until the next town, new and nondescript,
Approached with acres of dismantled cars.

At first, I didn't notice what a noise
  The weddings made
Each station that we stopped at: sun destroys
The interest of what's happening in the shade,

And down the long cool platforms whoops and skirls
I took for porters larking with the mails,
And went on reading. Once we started, though,
We passed them, grinning and pomaded, girls
In parodies of fashion, heels and veils,
All posed irresolutely, watching us go,

As if out on the end of an event
    Waving goodbye
To something that survived it. Struck, I leant
More promptly out next time, more curiously,
And saw it all again in different terms:
The fathers with broad belts under their suits
And seamy foreheads; mothers loud and fat;
An uncle shouting smut; and then the perms,
The nylon gloves and jewellery-substitutes,
The lemons, mauves, and olive-ochres that

Marked off the girls unreally from the rest.
    Yes, from cafés
And banquet-halls up yards, and bunting-dressed
Coach-party annexes, the wedding-days
Were coming to an end. All down the line
Fresh couples climbed aboard: the rest stood round;
The last confetti and advice were thrown,
And, as we moved, each face seemed to define
Just what it saw departing: children frowned
At something dull; fathers had never known

Success so huge and wholly farcical;
    The women shared
The secret like a happy funeral;

While girls, gripping their handbags tighter, stared
At a religious wounding. Free at last,
And loaded with the sum of all they saw,
We hurried towards London, shuffling gouts of steam.
Now fields were building-plots, and poplars cast
Long shadows over major roads, and for
Some fifty minutes, that in time would seem

Just long enough to settle hats and say
   I nearly died,
A dozen marriages got under way.
They watched the landscape, sitting side by side
– An Odeon went past, a cooling tower,
And someone running up to bowl – and none
Thought of the others they would never meet
Or how their lives would all contain this hour.
I thought of London spread out in the sun,
Its postal districts packed like squares of wheat:

There we were aimed. And as we raced across
   Bright knots of rail
Past standing Pullmans, walls of blackened moss
Came close, and it was nearly done, this frail
Travelling coincidence; and what it held
Stood ready to be loosed with all the power
That being changed can give. We slowed again,
And as the tightened brakes took hold, there swelled
A sense of falling, like an arrow-shower
Sent out of sight, somewhere becoming rain.

D. H. LAWRENCE
1885–1930

⸺ ∞∞∞ ⸺

David Herbert Lawrence was born in the Nottinghamshire village of Eastwood on 11 September 1885, the son of a miner and an ex-schoolteacher. It was not a happy marriage and Lawrence grew closer to his mother, who was determined to save her son from the pit and help him become a teacher. He won a scholarship to University College, Nottingham, and took up a teaching post in Croydon. His mother's death impaired his own health and he resigned his post, returning to Nottinghamshire. There he met Frieda von Richthofen, the wife of his old professor, six years his senior and the mother of three children.

In 1913 he published his novel *Sons and Lovers* and eloped to Germany with Frieda. At the beginning of the First World War they were in London, moving in literary and intellectual circles. However, in 1915 not only was his novel *The Rainbow* declared obscene but Frieda was suspected of being a German spy. They moved to Italy in 1919. Although the relationship was tempestuous and they lived in constant penury, Lawrence and Frieda still managed to travel widely, visiting Ceylon, Australia, America and Mexico, where Lawrence was diagnosed as having tuberculosis and given two years to live. The couple returned to Italy and, just before his death on 2 March 1930, Lawrence published what was to be his most controversial novel, *Lady Chatterley's Lover*.

72

SNAKE

A snake came to my water-trough
On a hot, hot day, and I in pyjamas for the heat,
To drink there.

In the deep, strange-scented shade of the great dark
     carob-tree
I came down the steps with my pitcher
And must wait, must stand and wait, for there he was at
     the trough before me.

He reached down from a fissure in the earth-wall in the
     gloom
And trailed his yellow-brown slackness soft-bellied down,
     over the edge of the stone trough
And rested his throat upon the stone bottom,
And where the water had dripped from the tap, in a small
     clearness,
He sipped with his straight mouth,
Softly drank through his straight gums, into his slack
     long body,
Silently.

Someone was before me at my water-trough,
And I, like a second comer, waiting.

D. H. Lawrence

He lifted his head from his drinking, as cattle do,
And looked at me vaguely, as drinking cattle do,
And flickered his two-forked tongue from his lips, and
    mused a moment,
And stooped and drank a little more,
Being earth-brown, earth-golden from the burning bowels
    of the earth
On the day of Sicilian July, with Etna smoking.

The voice of my education said to me
He must be killed,
For in Sicily the black, black snakes are innocent, the gold
    are venomous.

And voices in me said, If you were a man
You would take a stick and break him now, and finish him
    off.

But must I confess how I liked him,
How glad I was he had come like a guest in quiet, to drink at
    my water-trough
And depart peaceful, pacified, and thankless,
Into the burning bowels of this earth?

Was it cowardice, that I dared not kill him?
Was it perversity, that I longed to talk to him?
Was it humility, to feel so honoured?
I felt so honoured.

And yet those voices:
If you were not afraid, you would kill him!

And truly I was afraid, I was most afraid,
But even so, honoured still more
That he should seek my hospitality
From out the dark door of the secret earth.

He drank enough
And lifted his head, dreamily, as one who has drunken,
And flickered his tongue like a forked night on the air, so
    black,
Seeming to lick his lips,
And looked around like a god, unseeing, into the air,
And slowly turned his head.
And slowly, very slowly, as if thrice adream,
Proceeded to draw his slow length curving round
And climb again the broken bank of my wall-face.
And as he put his head into that dreadful hole,
And as he slowly drew up, snake-easing his shoulders,
    and entered farther,
A sort of horror, a sort of protest against his withdrawing
    into that horrid black hole,
Deliberately going into the blackness, and slowly drawing
    himself after,
Overcame me now his back was turned.

I looked round, I put down my pitcher,
I picked up a clumsy log
And threw it at the water-trough with a clatter.

I did not think it hit him,
But suddenly that part of him that was left behind
    convulsed in undignified haste,
Writhed like lightning, and was gone
Into the black hole, the earth-lipped fissure in the
    wall-front,
At which, in the intense still noon, I stared with fascination.

And immediately I regretted it.
I thought how paltry, how vulgar, what a mean act!
I despised myself and the voices of my accursed human
    education.

And I thought of the albatross,
And I wished he would come back, my snake.

For he seemed to me again like a king,
Like a king in exile, uncrowned in the underworld,
Now due to be crowned again.

And so, I missed my chance with one of the lords
Of life.
And I have something to expiate;
A pettiness.

EDWARD LEAR
1812–88

—— ⬯⬯⬯ ——

Lear was born on 12 May 1812, the twentieth child of a stockbroker who shortly afterwards went bankrupt. A sickly child, Lear suffered from epilepsy, asthma, bronchitis and, understandably, depression. However, he discovered that he had a talent for sketching flowers and birds and began to earn a living through his ornithological drawings. He was engaged by Lord Stanley, the 14th Earl of Derby, to draw the birds and animals in his menagerie, but Lear also started to write and illustrate nonsense poems to entertain the younger members of the Stanley family. In 1845 he published a collection of limericks, a form which he could not claim to have invented but which he certainly made his own. Accompanied by his companion Giorgio Cocali, he travelled extensively around the Mediterranean before settling in San Remo in 1870. 'The Owl and the Pussycat' was included in Lear's 1871 *Nonsense Songs*. He died in San Remo on 29 January 1888 and is buried there with Cocali and his beloved cat Foss.

Edward Lear

THE OWL AND THE PUSSY-CAT

The Owl and the Pussy-Cat went to sea
  In a beautiful pea-green boat,
They took some honey, and plenty of money
  Wrapped up in a five-pound note.
The Owl looked up to the stars above,
  And sang to a small guitar,
'O lovely Pussy! O Pussy, my love,
What a beautiful Pussy you are,
    You are,
    You are!
What a beautiful Pussy you are!'

Pussy said to Owl, 'You elegant fowl!
  How charmingly sweet you sing!
O let us be married! too long we have tarried
  But what shall we do for a ring?'
They sailed away, for a year and a day,
  To the land where the Bong-Tree grows,
And there in a wood a Piggy-wig stood,
With a ring at the end of his nose,
    His nose,
    His nose!
With a ring at the end of his nose.

'Dear Pig, are you willing to sell for one shilling
   Your ring?' Said the Piggy, 'I will.'
So they took it away, and were married next day
   By the Turkey who lives on the hill.
They dinèd on mince, and slices of quince,
   Which they ate with a runcible spoon;
And hand in hand, on the edge of the sand
   They danced by the light of the moon,
     The moon,
     The moon,
They danced by the light of the moon.

HENRY WADSWORTH LONGFELLOW
1807–82

———— ∞∞∞ ————

Longfellow was born on 27 February 1807 in Portland, Maine, into a wealthy American family who sent him to Bowdoin College in the neighbouring town of Brunswick. After graduating in 1825 he worked for a few months in his father's legal practice but the offer of the new Chair of Modern Languages at his alma mater was too tempting to resist and so Longfellow – still in his teens – became one of the youngest professors in academic history. He felt, however, that he needed to prepare himself for the job by travelling widely throughout Europe and steeping himself in all its different literatures. In 1836 he became Professor of Modern Languages and Belles Lettres at Harvard.

By the early 1840s Longfellow had established a formidable reputation as a poet and in the ensuing years his fame – especially as a writer of narrative poems – made him an international literary figure second only to Tennyson. He died on 24 March 1882, and two years after his death a bust was erected in Poets' Corner in Westminster Abbey by his admirers.

64

From THE SONG OF HIAWATHA

She had sent through all the village
Messengers with wands of willow,
As a sign of invitation,
As a token of the feasting;
And the wedding-guests assembled,
Clad in all their richest raiment,
Robes of fur and belts of wampum,
Splendid with their paint and plumage,
Beautiful with beads and tassels.
. . .

He was dressed in shirt of doeskin,
White and soft and fringed with ermine,
All inwrought with beads of wampum;
. . .

On his head were plumes of swan's down,
On his heels were tails of foxes,
In one hand a fan of feathers,
And a pipe was in the other.
. . .

Looking still at Hiawatha,
Looking at fair Laughing Water,
Sang he softly, sang in this wise:
    'Onaway! Awake, beloved!
Thou the wild-flower of the forest!
Thou the wild-bird of the prairie!

Thou with eyes so soft and fawn-like!
  'If thou only lookest at me,
I am happy, I am happy,
As the lilies of the prairie,
When they feel the dew upon them!
  'Sweet thy breath is as the fragrance
Of the wild-flowers in the morning,
As their fragrance is at evening,
In the Moon when leaves are falling.'
. . .
'True is all Iagoo tells us;
I have seen it in a vision,
Seen the great canoe with pinions,
Seen the people with white faces,
Seen the coming of this bearded
People of the wooden vessel
From the regions of the morning,
From the shining land of Wabun.
. . .
  I beheld, too, in that vision
All the secrets of the future,
Of the distant days that shall be.
I beheld the westward marches
Of the unknown, crowded nations.
All the land was full of people,
Restless, struggling, toiling, striving,
Speaking many tongues, yet feeling
But one heart-beat in their bosoms.
In the woodlands rang their axes,
Smoked their towns in all the valleys,

Over all the lakes and rivers
Rushed their great canoes of thunder.
Then a darker, drearier vision
Passed before me, vague and cloud-like.
I beheld our nations scattered,
All forgetful of my counsels,
Weakened, warring with each other;
Saw the remnants of our people
Sweeping westward, wild and woeful,
Like the cloud-rack of a tempest,
Like the withered leaves of autumn!'
. . .

On the shore stood Hiawatha,
Turned and waved his hand at parting;
On the clear and luminous water
Launched his birch-canoe for sailing,
From the pebbles of the margin
Shoved it forth into the water;
Whispered to it: 'Westward! westward!'
And with speed it darted forward.
And the evening sun descending
Set the clouds on fire with redness,
Burned the broad sky, like a prairie,
Left upon the level water
One long track and trail of splendour,
Down whose stream, as down a river,
Westward, westward Hiawatha
Sailed into the fiery sunset,
Sailed into the purple vapours,
Sailed into the dusk of evening.

90

A PSALM OF LIFE

WHAT THE HEART OF THE YOUNG MAN

SAID TO THE PSALMIST

Tell me not, in mournful numbers,
  'Life is but an empty dream!'
For the soul is dead that slumbers,
  And things are not what they seem.

Life is real! Life is earnest!
  And the grave is not its goal;
'Dust thou art, to dust returnest'
  Was not spoken of the soul.

Not enjoyment, and not sorrow,
  Is our destined end or way;
But to act, that each to-morrow
  Find us farther than to-day.

Art is long, and Time is fleeting,
  And our hearts, though stout and brave,
Still, like muffled drums, are beating
  Funeral marches to the grave.

In the world's broad field of battle,
  In the bivouac of Life,
Be not like dumb, driven cattle!
  Be a hero in the strife!

Trust no Future, howe'er pleasant!
  Let the dead Past bury its dead!
Act – act in the living Present!
  Heart within, and God o'erhead!

Lives of great men all remind us
  We can make our lives sublime,
And, departing, leave behind us
  Footprints on the sands of time;

Footprints, that perhaps another,
  Sailing o'er life's solemn main,
A forlorn and shipwrecked brother,
  Seeing, shall take heart again.

Let us, then, be up and doing,
  With a heart for any fate;
Still achieving, still pursuing,
  Learn to labour and to wait.

JOHN GILLESPIE MAGEE
1922–41

———— ∞∞ ————

John Gillespie Magee (Jr) was born on 9 June 1922 in Shanghai, the son of an American father and of a British mother who were Episcopalian missionaries. He was sent to school at Rugby where he developed a keen interest in poetry and in particular in the life and work of former Rugby pupil Rupert Brooke. Like Brooke, to whom he dedicated a sonnet, he won the Rugby Poetry Prize at the age of sixteen. At the approach of the Second World War John was sent by his worried father to America to prepare for entrance to Yale, but the boy considered that Britain was his home. In the summer of 1940 he turned down a Yale scholarship in order to enlist in the RAF, but the US State Department refused to carry out the necessary paperwork and so Magee joined the Canadian Air Force instead. In June 1941 he was posted to a base in Wales where he flew Spitfires. He was then transferred to 412 Squadron based at Wellingore in Lincolnshire, and took part in several missions over occupied Europe. He was killed on 11 December 1941, ironically not by enemy fire but when his Spitfire collided with another plane fourteen hundred feet above RAF Cranwell. He was just nineteen years old.

His two most famous poems are 'Per Ardua', a tribute to the 'Few' of the Battle of Britain, and 'High Flight'. The perennial popularity of the latter poem was emphasised when President Reagan quoted some of its lines following the Challenger Space Shuttle disaster in 1986.

John Gillespie Magee

HIGH FLIGHT

Oh, I have slipped the surly bonds of earth
And danced the skies on laughter-silvered wings;
Sunward I've climbed and joined the tumbling mirth
Of sun-split clouds – and done a hundred things
You have not dreamed of; wheeled and soared and swung
High in the sun-lit silence. Hovering there
I've chased the shouting wind along, and flung
My eager craft through footless halls of air;
Up, up the long, delirious, burning blue
I've topped the wind-swept heights with easy grace,
Where never lark nor even eagle flew;
And while, with silent lifting mind I've trod
The high untrespassed sanctity of space,
Put out my hand, and touched the face of God.

CHRISTOPHER MARLOWE
1564–93

———— ∞∞∞ ————

Marlowe was born in Canterbury, the son of a shoemaker, and was educated at King's School, Canterbury, and Corpus Christi, Cambridge. For all his academic qualifications he was a man who often found himself on the wrong side of the law and was involved in a number of violent incidents, notably a fatal street brawl in 1589 and an occasion when he was deported from the Netherlands for passing forged gold coins. Yet as a poet and playwright he was highly regarded, influencing some of Shakespeare's early work. He also found time, allegedly, to act as a government agent in the murky world of Elizabethan espionage. At the time of his mysterious and violent death, on 30 May 1593, he was facing a charge of holding blasphemous opinions.

There are varying accounts of how and why Marlowe died. One witness testified that he was stabbed by a serving-man, 'a rival of his in his lewde love'. Another stated that he had tried to knife a man called Ingram during an argument at the gaming-tables, and Ingram retaliated with such force that people saw Marlowe's 'brains comming out at the dagger's point'. The burial register at St Nicholas Church, Deptford, where Marlowe is buried, suggests yet another suspect – one Francis Frazer.

Christopher Marlowe

THE PASSIONATE SHEPHERD TO HIS LOVE

Come live with me and be my Love,
And we will all the pleasures prove
That hills and valleys, dales and fields,
And all the craggy mountains yields.

There we will sit upon the rocks
And see the shepherds feed their flocks,
By shallow rivers, to whose falls
Melodious birds sing madrigals.

And I will make thee beds of roses
And a thousand fragrant posies,
A cap of flowers, and a kirtle
Embroider'd all with leaves of myrtle.

A gown made of the finest wool,
Which from our pretty lambs we pull,
Fair lined slippers for the cold,
With buckles of the purest gold.

A belt of straw and ivy buds
With coral clasps and amber studs:
And if these pleasures may thee move,
Come live with me and be my Love.

Thy silver dishes for thy meat
As precious as the gods do eat,
Shall on an ivory table be
Prepared each day for thee and me.

The shepherd swains shall dance and sing
For thy delight each May-morning:
If these delights thy mind may move,
Then live with me and be my Love.

ANDREW MARVELL
1621–78

——— ∞∞ ———

Marvell, the son of a clergyman, was born on 31 March 1621 just a few miles from the mouth of the Humber at Winestead-in-Holderness. He was educated at Hull Grammar School and Trinity College, Cambridge, where he graduated in 1639. After travelling through Europe for four years he settled in 1647 in London, where he both moved in Royalist circles and wrote an ode in celebration of Cromwell's return from his successful campaign in Ireland. Cromwell employed Marvell as his ward's tutor and was generous in his favours, virtually making him the unofficial Poet Laureate. At Cromwell's death in 1658 Marvell was understandably distraught, but he survived the restoration of the monarchy to serve as MP for Hull. In 1663 he became private secretary to the Earl of Carlisle and vigorously attacked the new regime for its financial and sexual corruption. Although during his lifetime Marvell was regarded primarily as a satirist, T. S. Eliot has called for him to be reappraised as a lyric poet.

Marvell died on 18 August 1678 at his home in Great Russell Street, London.

22

TO HIS COY MISTRESS

Had we but world enough, and time,
This coyness, Lady, were no crime.
We would sit down, and think which way
To walk, and pass our long love's day.
Thou by the Indian Ganges' side
Shouldst rubies find: I by the tide
Of Humber would complain. I would
Love you ten years before the Flood,
And you should, if you please, refuse
Till the conversion of the Jews.
My vegetable love should grow
Vaster than empires, and more slow.
An hundred years should go to praise
Thine eyes, and on thy forehead gaze;
Two hundred to adore each breast,
But thirty thousand to the rest.
An age at least to every part,
And the last age should show your heart.
For, Lady, you deserve this state,
Nor would I love at lower rate.
   But at my back I always hear
Time's wingèd chariot hurrying near;
And yonder all before us lie
Deserts of vast eternity.
Thy beauty shall no more be found,

Nor, in my marble vault, shall sound
My echoing song: then worms shall try
That long preserved virginity,
And your quaint honour turn to dust,
And into ashes all my lust.
The grave's a fine and private place,
But none, I think, do there embrace.
   Now, therefore, while the youthful hue
Sits on thy skin like morning dew,
And while thy willing soul transpires
At every pore with instant fires,
Now let us sport us while we may,
And now, like amorous birds of prey,
Rather at once our time devour,
Than languish in his slow-chapt power.
Let us roll all our strength, and all
Our sweetness, up into one ball,
And tear our pleasures with rough strife
Thorough the iron gates of life:
Thus, though we cannot make our sun
Stand still, yet we will make him run.

JOHN MASEFIELD
1878–1967

Masefield was born on 1 June 1878 in Ledbury, Here-fordshire, the son of a solicitor who suffered a nervous breakdown because of financial problems when the boy was six years old. Masefield went to sea at the age of thirteen, where he too suffered a nervous collapse. He jumped ship in New York in 1895, lived as a vagrant and then returned to London in 1897 to work as a bank clerk. In 1904 he joined the *Manchester Guardian* as a journalist. His early poems were inspired by his years in the Merchant Navy, and his close friendship with W. B. Yeats inspired him to persevere. After marrying in 1902, Masefield moved from London's Marylebone Road to Lollingdon in the Thames Valley. During the First World War he served with the Red Cross at Gallipoli, and during the 1920s his reputation steadily grew until he succeeded Bridges as Poet Laureate in 1930. Five years later he was awarded the Order of Merit, and in the 1960s he was made a Companion of Literature amongst other honours.

John Masefield

CARGOES

Quinquireme of Nineveh from distant Ophir
Rowing home to haven in sunny Palestine,
With a cargo of ivory,
And apes and peacocks,
Sandalwood, cedarwood, and sweet white wine.

Stately Spanish galleon coming from the Isthmus,
Dipping through the Tropics by the palm-green shores,
With a cargo of diamonds,
Emeralds, amethysts,
Topazes, and cinnamon, and gold moidores.

Dirty British coaster with a salt-caked smoke-stack
Butting through the Channel in the mad March days,
With a cargo of Tyne coal,
Road-rail, pig-lead,
Firewood, iron-ware, and cheap tin trays.

10

SEA FEVER

I must down to the seas again, to the lonely sea and the sky,
And all I ask is a tall ship and a star to steer her by,
And the wheel's kick and the wind's song and the white
    sail's shaking,
And a grey mist on the sea's face and a grey dawn breaking.

I must down to the seas again, for the call of the running
    tide
Is a wild call and a clear call that may not be denied;
And all I ask is a windy day with the white clouds flying,
And the flung spray and the blown spume, and the sea-gulls
    crying.

I must down to the seas again, to the vagrant gypsy life,
To the gull's way and the whale's way where the wind's like
    a whetted knife;
And all I ask is a merry yarn from a laughing fellow-rover,
And quiet sleep and a sweet dream when the long trick's
    over.

89

From REYNARD THE FOX

The fox knew well as he ran the dark,
That the headlong hounds were past their mark;
They had missed his swerve and had overrun,
But their devilish play was not yet done.

For a minute he ran and heard no sound,
Then a whimper came from a questing hound,
Then a 'This way, beauties,' and then 'Leu, Leu,'
The floating laugh of the horn that blew.
Then the cry again, and the crash and rattle
Of the shrubs burst back as they ran to battle,
Till the wood behind seemed risen from root,
Crying and crashing, to give pursuit,
Till the trees seemed hounds and the air seemed cry,
And the earth so far that he needs but die,
Die where he reeled in the woodland dim,
With a hound's white grips in the spine of him.
For one more burst he could spurt, and then
Wait for the teeth, and the wrench, and men.

He made his spurt for the Mourne End rocks.
The air blew rank with the taint of fox;
The yews gave way to a greener space
Of great stones strewn in a grassy place.

And there was his earth at the great grey shoulder,
Sunk in the ground, of a granite boulder.
A dry, deep burrow with rocky roof,
Proof against crowbars, terrier-proof,
Life to the dying, rest for bones.

The earth was stopped; it was filled with stones.

Then, for a moment, his courage failed,
His eyes looked up as his body quailed,
Then the coming of death, which all things dread,
Made him run for the wood ahead.

The taint of fox was rank on the air,
He knew, as he ran, there were foxes there.
His strength was broken, his heart was bursting,
His bones were rotten, his throat was thirsting;
His feet were reeling, his brush was thick
From dragging the mud, and his brain was sick.

He thought as he ran of his old delight
In the wood in the moon in an April night,
His happy hunting, his winter loving,
The smells of things in the midnight roving,
The look of his dainty-nosing, red,
Clean-felled dam with her footpad's tread;
Of his sire, so swift, so game, so cunning,
With craft in his brain and power of running;
Their fights of old when his teeth drew blood,
Now he was sick, with his coat all mud.

John Masefield

He crossed the covert, he crawled the bank,
To a meuse in the thorns, and there he sank,
With his ears flexed back and his teeth shown white,
In a rat's resolve for a dying bite.

JOHN MILTON
1608–74

Milton was born on 9 December 1608 in Cheapside, London, the son of an eminent scrivener. He was educated at home by the Puritan Thomas Young, who gave his pupil a strong love of liberty. In his fifteenth year Milton went to St Paul's School where his hunger for knowledge led to long reading sessions late at night, a habit which may have contributed to his later blindness. After only a year at Christ's College, Cambridge, he joined his retired father in Colnbrook, Buckinghamshire, where he wrote amongst other things his famous masque 'Comus'.

Milton then began to travel, meeting the astronomer Galileo during a visit to Florence between 1637 and 1639. After his marriage in 1642 to Mary Powell, a member of a Royalist family, Milton was denounced for publishing a pamphlet which seemed to advocate sexual experience rather than a chaste upbringing as preparation for married life. During the Civil War Milton's sympathies were on the side of Parliament, and he was appointed Latin Secretary to the newly formed Council of State in 1649. By 1652, the year his wife died giving birth to the third of their daughters, he had become totally blind.

After the Restoration in 1660 Milton went into hiding. He was discovered and arrested, but only fined and released from custody. Settling in London's Bunhill Row with his third wife, he began to write poetry again. He completed *Paradise Lost* in 1663. He died of gout on 8 November 1674 and was buried alongside his father in St Giles, Cripplegate.

94

From PARADISE LOST, BOOK III

Hail, holy light, offspring of Heav'n first-born,
Or of th'Eternal Coeternal beam
May I express thee unblam'd? since God is light,
And never but in unapproached light
Dwelt from Eternitie, dwelt then in thee,
Bright effluence of bright essence increate.
Or hear'st thou rather pure Ethereal stream,
Whose fountain who shall tell? before the Sun,
Before the Heavens thou wert, and at the voice
Of God, as with a Mantle didst invest
The rising world of waters dark and deep,
Won from the void and formless infinite.
Thee I revisit now with bolder wing,
Escap't the Stygian pool, though long detain'd
In that obscure sojourn, while in my flight
Through utter and through middle darkness borne
With other notes than to th'Orphean Lyre
I sung of Chaos and Eternal Night,
Taught by the heavenly Muse to venture down
The dark descent, and up to reascend,
Though hard and rare: thee I revisit safe,
And feel thy sovran vital Lamp; but thou
Revisit'st not these eyes, that rowle in vain
To find thy piercing ray, and find no dawn;
So thick a drop serene hath quenched their Orbs,

Or dim suffusion veil'd. Yet not the more
Cease I to wander where the Muses haunt,
Clear Spring, or shadie Grove, or Sunnie Hill,
Smit with the love of sacred song; but chief
Thee Sion and the flowrie Brooks beneath
That wash thy hallow'd feet, and warbling flow,
Nightly I visit: nor sometimes forget
Those other two equal'd with me in Fate,
So were I equal'd with them in renown,
Blind Thamyris and blind Maeonides,
And Tiresias and Phineus, Prophets old.
Then feed on thoughts, that voluntarie move
Harmonious numbers; as the wakeful Bird
Sings darkling, and in shadiest Covert hid
Tunes her nocturnal Note. Thus with the Year
Seasons return; but not to me returns
Day, or the sweet approach of Ev'n or Morn
Or sight of vernal bloom, or Summer's Rose,
Or flocks, or herds, or human face divine;
But cloud instead, and ever-during dark
Surrounds me, from the cheerful waies of men
Cut off, and for the Book of knowledge fair
Presented with a Universal blank
Of Nature's works to mee expung'd and ras'd,
And wisdome at one entrance quite shut out.
So much the rather thou, Celestial light,
Shine inward, and the mind through all her powers
Irradiate; there plant eyes, all mist from thence
Purge and disperse, that I may see and tell
Of things invisible to mortal sight.

SIR HENRY NEWBOLT
1862–1938

———— ❦ ————

Henry John Newbolt was born on 6 June 1862, the son of a vicar, and was educated at Clifton College, Bristol, a time and place he later immortalised in the poem 'Clifton Chapel'. He went up to Corpus Christi College, Oxford, before embarking on a successful career as a lawyer and naval historian. By 1897 he had also achieved great popularity as a poet, selling that year twenty-one thousand copies of his collection *Admirals All* which contains 'Drake's Drum' and 'He Fell Among Thieves'. During the First World War Newbolt was appointed Controller of Telecommunication, made the official war historian and knighted in 1915. After the war Newbolt continued his active role in public life, serving on numerous committees including the Royal Literary Fund. His work found a new public after Charles Stanford set some of his sea-songs to music.

52

VITAÏ LAMPADA

There's a breathless hush in the Close to-night –
 Ten to make and the match to win –
A bumping pitch and a blinding light,
 An hour to play and the last man in.
And it's not for the sake of a ribboned coat,
 Or the selfish hope of a season's fame,
But his Captain's hand on his shoulder smote –
 'Play up! play up! and play the game!'

The sand of the desert is sodden red, –
 Red with the wreck of a square that broke; –
The Gatling's jammed and the Colonel dead,
 And the regiment blind with dust and smoke.
The river of death has brimmed his banks,
 And England's far, and Honour a name,
But the voice of a schoolboy rallies the ranks:
 'Play up! play up! and play the game!'

 This is the word that year by year,
 While in her place the School is set,
 Every one of her sons must hear,
 And none that hears it dare forget.
 This they all with a joyful mind
 Bear through life like a torch in flame,
 And falling fling to the host behind –
 'Play up! play up! and play the game!'

79

HE FELL AMONG THIEVES

'Ye have robbed,' said he, 'ye have slaughtered and made
    an end,
    Take your ill-got plunder, and bury the dead:
What will ye more of your guest and sometime friend?'
    'Blood for our blood,' they said.

He laughed: 'If one may settle the score for five,
    I am ready; but let the reckoning stand till day:
I have loved the sunlight as dearly as any alive.'
    'You shall die at dawn,' said they.

He flung his empty revolver down the slope,
    He climbed alone to the Eastward edge of the trees;
All night long in a dream untroubled of hope
    He brooded, clasping his knees.

He did not hear the monotonous roar that fills
    The ravine where the Yassin river sullenly flows;
He did not see the starlight on the Laspur hills,
    Or the far Afghan snows.

He saw the April noon on his books aglow,
    The wistaria trailing in at the window wide;
He heard his father's voice from the terrace below
    Calling him down to ride.

Sir Henry Newbolt

He saw the grey little church across the park,
  The mounds that hide the loved and honoured dead;
The Norman arch, the chancel softly dark,
  The brasses black and red.

He saw the School Close, sunny and green,
  The runner beside him, the stand by the parapet wall,
The distant tape, and the crowd roaring between
  His own name over all.

He saw the dark wainscot and timbered roof,
  The long tables, and the faces merry and keen;
The College Eight and their trainer dining aloof,
  The Dons on the dais serene.

He watched the liner's stem ploughing the foam,
  He felt her trembling speed and the thrash of her screw;
He heard her passengers' voices talking of home,
  He saw the flag she flew.

And now it was dawn. He rose strong on his feet,
  And strode to his ruined camp below the wood;
He drank the breath of the morning cool and sweet;
  His murderers round him stood.

Light on the Laspur hills was broadening fast,
  The blood-red snow-peaks chilled to a dazzling white:
He turned, and saw the golden circle at last,
  Cut by the Eastern height.

'O glorious Life, Who dwellest in earth and sun,
　I have lived, I praise and adore Thee.'

                                        A sword swept.

Over the pass the voices one by one
　Faded, and the hill slept.

ALFRED NOYES
1880–1958

Alfred Noyes was born in Wolverhampton in 1880, the son of a wealthy grocer, and was educated at various schools in Wales before going up to Exeter College, Oxford. A powerful oarsman, he excelled at sport but missed out on sitting his Finals in 1902 as he was in London, arranging the publication of his first book of poems, *The Loom of Years*. The young poet was hailed by the venerable George Meredith and his epic poem 'Drake', serialised in *Blackwood's Magazine* between 1906 and 1908, proved so popular that Noyes found he could make a decent living as a professional writer.

Working for the Foreign Office during the First World War he became involved in the prosecution of the Irish Nationalist Sir Roger Casement, whose position in his trial for treason was worsened by the revelation in his diaries of various homosexual encounters. In the 1920s Noyes became embroiled in controversy with W. B. Yeats over the Casement affair, and as a self-appointed adversary of modernism and what he considered to be immorality he led the campaign against James Joyce's *Ulysses*. Having spent the Second World War in America, he settled with his second wife on the Isle of Wight where he died in 1958. Long out of fashion, perhaps Noyes will return to favour one day.

13

THE HIGHWAYMAN

The wind was a torrent of darkness upon the gusty
    trees,
The moon was a ghostly galleon tossed upon cloudy
    seas,
The road was a ribbon of moonlight looping the purple
    moor,
And the highwayman came riding –
Riding – riding –
The highwayman came riding, up to the old inn door.

He'd a French cocked hat on his forehead, and a bunch
    of lace at his chin;
He'd a coat of the claret velvet, and breeches of fine
    doe-skin.
They fitted with never a wrinkle; his boots were up to
    his thigh!
And he rode with a jewelled twinkle –
His rapier hilt a-twinkle –
His pistol butts a-twinkle, under the jewelled sky.

Over the cobbles he clattered and clashed in the dark
  inn-yard,
He tapped with his whip on the shutters, but all was
  locked and barred,
He whistled a tune to the window, and who should be
  waiting there
But the landlord's black-eyed daughter –
Bess, the landlord's daughter –
Plaiting a dark red love-knot into her long black hair.

Dark in the dark old inn-yard a stable-wicket creaked
Where Tim the ostler listened – his face was white and
  peaked –
His eyes were hollows of madness, his hair like mouldy
  hay,
But he loved the landlord's daughter –
The landlord's black-eyed daughter;
Dumb as a dog he listened, and he heard the robber
  say:

'One kiss, my bonny sweetheart; I'm after a prize
  tonight,
But I shall be back with the yellow gold before the
  morning light.
Yet if they press me sharply, and harry me through the
  day,
Then look for me by moonlight,
Watch for me by moonlight,
I'll come to thee by moonlight, though hell should bar
  the way.'

He stood upright in the stirrups; he scarce could reach
her hand,
But she loosened her hair in the casement! His face
burnt like a brand
As the sweet black waves of perfume came tumbling
o'er his breast,
Then he kissed its waves in the moonlight
(O sweet black waves in the moonlight!),
And he tugged at his reins in the moonlight, and
galloped away to the west.

He did not come in the dawning; he did not come at
noon.
And out of the tawny sunset, before the rise of the
moon,
When the road was a gypsy's ribbon over the purple
moor,
The redcoat troops came marching –
Marching – marching –
King George's men came marching, up to the old inn-door.

They said no word to the landlord; they drank his ale
instead,
But they gagged his daughter and bound her to the foot
of her narrow bed.
Two of them knelt at her casement, with muskets by
their side;
There was Death at every window,
And Hell at one dark window,
For Bess could see, through her casement, the road that
he would ride.

They had bound her up at attention, with many a
    sniggering jest!
They had tied a rifle beside her, with the barrel beneath
    her breast!
'Now keep good watch!' and they kissed her. She heard
    the dead man say,
'Look for me by moonlight,
Watch for me by moonlight,
I'll come to thee by moonlight, though Hell should bar
    the way.'

She twisted her hands behind her, but all the knots held
    good!
She writhed her hands till her fingers were wet with
    sweat or blood!
They stretched and strained in the darkness, and the
    hours crawled by like years,
Till, on the stroke of midnight,
Cold on the stroke of midnight,
The tip of one finger touched it! The trigger at least was
    hers!

The tip of one finger touched it, she strove no more for
    the rest;
Up, she stood up at attention, with the barrel beneath
    her breast.
She would not risk their hearing, she would not strive again,
For the road lay bare in the moonlight,
Blank and bare in the moonlight,
And the blood in her veins, in the moonlight, throbbed
    to her love's refrain.

Tlot tlot, tlot tlot! Had they heard it? The horse-hooves,
   ringing clear;
Tlot tlot, tlot tlot, in the distance! Were they deaf that
   they did not hear?
Down the ribbon of moonlight, over the brow of the
   hill,
The highwayman came riding –
Riding – riding –
The redcoats looked to their priming! She stood up
   straight and still.

Tlot tlot, in the frosty silence! Tlot tlot, in the echoing
   night!
Nearer he came and nearer! Her face was like a light!
Her eyes grew wide for a moment, she drew one last
   deep breath,
Then her finger moved in the moonlight –
Her musket shattered the moonlight –
Shattered her breast in the moonlight and warned him –
   with her death.

He turned, he spurred to the West; he did not know
   who stood
Bowed, with her head o'er the casement, drenched in
   her own red blood!
Not till the dawn did he hear it, and his face grew grey
   to hear
How Bess, the landlord's daughter,
The landlord's black-eyed daughter,
Had watched for her love in the moonlight, and died in
   the darkness there.

Back, he spurred like a madman, shrieking a curse to
the sky,
With the white road smoking behind him and his rapier
brandished high!
Blood-red were his spurs in the golden noon, wine-red
was his velvet coat
When they shot him down in the highway,
Down like a dog in the highway,
And he lay in his blood in the highway, with the bunch
of lace at his throat.

And still on a winter's night, they say, when the wind is
in the trees,
When the moon is a ghostly galleon tossed upon cloudy
seas,
When the road is a gypsy's ribbon looping the purple
moor,
The highwayman comes riding –
Riding – riding –
The highwayman comes riding, up to the old inn-door.

Over the cobbles he clatters and clangs in the dark inn-
yard,
He taps with his whip on the shutters, but all is locked
and barred,
He whistles a tune to the window, and who should be
waiting there
But the landlord's black-eyed daughter –
Bess, the landlord's daughter –
Plaiting a dark red love-knot into her long black hair.

WILFRED OWEN
1893–1918

⸺⸏⸺

Wilfred Edward Salter Owen was born on 18 March 1893 in the Shropshire town of Oswestry, the son of a station-master. Educated at Birkenhead Institute and Shrewsbury Technical College, he was encouraged by his mother to read the great poets and so develop his own voice. After London University he went to Bordeaux to teach English at the Berlitz School, and so was in France at the outbreak of the First World War.

He enlisted in 1915, and in the summer of 1916 became a second lieutenant in the 2nd Battalion of the Manchester Regiment. His experience of the realities of war enabled Owen to forge his own style of poetry and he became one of the most celebrated poets of the First World War. Sent to Craiglockhart Hospital on the outskirts of Edinburgh in 1917 to recover from shellshock, he met and befriended fellow poet Siegfried Sassoon, who introduced him to Robert Graves.

In September 1918 Owen returned to the Front and was awarded the Military Cross, only to be killed by machine-gun fire just a week before the Armistice. Despite his relatively small output (he only had six poems published during his lifetime) his reputation gathered momentum after his death, influencing many of the poets of the 1930s. Benjamin Britten included some of Owen's poetry in his 1961 *War Requiem*.

DULCE ET DECORUM EST

Bent double, like old beggars under sacks,
Knock-kneed, coughing like hags, we cursed through
    sludge,
Till on the haunting flares we turned our backs
And towards our distant rest began to trudge.
Men marched asleep. Many had lost their boots
But limped on, blood-shod. All went lame; all blind;
Drunk with fatigue; deaf even to the hoots
Of tired, outstripped Five-Nines that dropped behind.

Gas! Gas! Quick, boys! – An ecstasy of fumbling,
Fitting the clumsy helmets just in time;
But someone still was yelling out and stumbling
And flound'ring like a man in fire or lime . . .
Dim, through the misty panes and thick green light,
As under a green sea, I saw him drowning.

In all my dreams, before my helpless sight,
He plunges at me, guttering, choking, drowning.

If in some smothering dreams you too could pace
Behind the wagon that we flung him in,
And watch the white eyes writhing in his face,
His hanging face, like a devil's sick of sin;

Wilfred Owen

If you could hear, at every jolt, the blood
Come gargling from the froth-corrupted lungs,
Obscene as cancer, bitter as the cud
Of vile, incurable sores on innocent tongues, –
My friend, you would not tell with such high zest
To children ardent for some desperate glory,
The old Lie: Dulce et decorum est
Pro patria mori.

ANTHEM FOR DOOMED YOUTH

What passing-bells for these who die as cattle?
  Only the monstrous anger of the guns.
  Only the stuttering rifles' rapid rattle
Can patter out their hasty orisons.
No mockeries now for them; no prayers nor bells,
  Nor any voice of mourning save the choirs, –
The shrill, demented choirs of wailing shells;
  And bugles calling for them from sad shires.

What candles may be held to speed them all?
  Not in the hands of boys, but in their eyes
Shall shine the holy glimmers of good-byes.
  The pallor of girls' brows shall be their pall;
Their flowers the tenderness of patient minds,
And each slow dusk a drawing-down of blinds.

86

FUTILITY

Move him into the sun –
Gently its touch awoke him once,
At home, whispering of fields unsown.
Always it woke him, even in France,
Until this morning and this snow.
If anything might rouse him now
The kind old sun will know.

Think how it wakes the seeds, –
Woke, once, the clays of a cold star.
Are limbs, so dear-achieved, are sides,
Full-nerved – still warm – too hard to stir?
Was it for this the clay grew tall?
– O what made fatuous sunbeams toil
To break earth's sleep at all?

CHRISTINA ROSSETTI
1830–94

Christina Rossetti was born on 5 December 1830, the youngest of the four children of Gabriele Rossetti, Professor of Italian at King's College, London, and of Frances Polidori, the sister of Byron's secretary. Educated mainly at home by her mother, she began writing poetry in her teens, initially under a pseudonym. However, after the publication of 'Goblin Market' and other poems in 1862, she became known for her work under her own name. Devoutly High Anglican, she rejected two suitors on religious grounds and began an affair with the married painter and poet William Bell Scott, but she was destined to remain unmarried.

For many years Rossetti worked at the Highgate Penitentiary, helping women who had turned to prostitution in hard times, but an attack of Graves disease, a disorder of the thyroid gland which leads to a swelling of the face, caused her to withdraw from public life. Although she remained a member of the Portfolio Society and continued to receive a number of women friends, her former admirer, the poet Charles Bagot Cayley, was the only man, outside her family, permitted to visit her at home at 30 Torrington Square in Bloomsbury, where she died on 29 December 1894.

9

REMEMBER ME

Remember me when I am gone away,
 Gone far away into the silent land;
 When you can no more hold me by the hand,
Nor I half turn to go yet turning stay.
Remember me when no more day by day
 You tell me of our future that you planned:
 Only remember me; you understand
It will be late to counsel then or pray.
Yet if you should forget me for a while
 And afterwards remember, do not grieve:
 For if the darkness and corruption leave
 A vestige of the thoughts that once I had,
Better by far you should forget and smile
 Than that you should remember and be sad.

SIEGFRIED SASSOON
1886–1967

Siegfried Sassoon was born on 8 September 1886 into a wealthy family and educated at Marlborough and Clare College, Cambridge. His youth was spent in the pleasures of cricket and fox-hunting although his mother encouraged his poetic leanings. Wearying of country pursuits, he decided in 1913 to send his work to Edward Marsh, the mentor of the leading young poets of the day, and through Marsh he met Rupert Brooke, W. B. Yeats and Edward Thomas. He described his encounter with Brooke as 'rather like a Lower Fifth Form boy talking to the Head of the School'.

During the First World War he served as a captain in the Royal Welch Fusiliers, winning the Military Cross, but his initial idealism gave way to a bitter disillusionment as he experienced the realities of war. He threw his medal into the River Mersey and declared that he would no longer obey orders. At Craiglockhart Hospital near Edinburgh he met Wilfred Owen and publicly spoke out against the war, yet returned to serve with his regiment through the final stages of hostilities.

During the 1920s and 1930s his poetry became increasingly religious. He joined the Labour Party's Pacifist Movement and was appointed Literary Editor of the *Daily Herald*. Despite a series of homosexual affairs, he briefly married and fathered a much-loved son. In 1951 he was awarded a CBE and six years later received the Queen's Medal for Poetry. In old age he became a melancholy semi-recluse at his home, Heytesbury House in Wiltshire, where he died, a week short of his eighty-first birthday, on 1 September 1967.

Siegfried Sassoon

EVERYONE SANG

Everyone suddenly burst out singing;
And I was filled with such delight
As prisoned birds must find in freedom
Winging wildly across the white
Orchards and dark-green fields; on; on; and out of sight.

Everyone's voice was suddenly lifted,
And beauty came like the setting sun.
My heart was shaken with tears; and horror
Drifted away . . . O but every one
Was a bird; and the song was wordless; the singing will
    never be done.

WILLIAM SHAKESPEARE
1564–1616

---◦∞∞◦---

Shakespeare is perhaps the most famous writer of all time. He was born on 23 April 1564 in Stratford-upon-Avon, the son of a glover and wool-dealer. After being educated at King's New School, Stratford, in 1582 he married Anne Hathaway, eight years his senior. A daughter, Susanna, was born in 1583, followed by the twins Hamnet and Judith. By 1587, Shakespeare was in London, making a name for himself at the Blackfriars Theatre as both actor and playwright. For ten years he was lessee of the Globe Theatre, his celebrated 'Wooden O', on Bankside until, at the age of forty, he retired from public life and returned to Stratford as a wealthy, self-made man.

There have been claims that Shakespeare, a man of relatively humble origins, could not have been the author of such a dazzling collection of work. Other candidates, notably Francis Bacon, have been proposed but nothing has been proved. There has also been recent speculation that he was involved in the shadowy world of Elizabethan espionage, and theories continue to be put forward to explain the gaps in our knowledge of his life.

William Shakespeare

SONNET 18

Shall I compare thee to a summer's day?
Thou art more lovely and more temperate:
Rough winds do shake the darling buds of May,
And summer's lease hath all too short a date:
Sometime too hot the eye of heaven shines,
And often is his gold complexion dimm'd;
And every fair from fair sometime declines,
By chance, or nature's changing course, untrimm'd;
But thy eternal summer shall not fade
Nor lose possession of that fair thou ow'st,
Nor shall Death brag thou wand'rest in his shade
When in eternal lines to time thou grow'st:
   So long as men can breathe or eyes can see,
   So long lives this, and this gives life to thee.

20

SONNET 116

Let me not to the marriage of true minds
Admit impediments. Love is not love
Which alters when it alteration finds,
Or bends with the remover to remove:
O no! it is an ever-fixèd mark,
That looks on tempests and is never shaken;
It is the star to every wandering bark,
Whose worth's unknown, although his height be taken.
Love's not Time's fool, though rosy lips and cheeks
Within his bending sickle's compass come;
Love alters not with his brief hours and weeks,
But bears it out even to the edge of doom:
     If this be error and upon me proved,
     I never writ, nor no man ever loved.

55

WINTER
From LOVE'S LABOUR'S LOST

When icicles hang by the wall,
   And Dick, the shepherd, blows his nail,
And Tom bears logs into the hall,
   And milk comes frozen home in pail,
When blood is nipp'd, and ways be foul,
Then nightly sings the staring owl:
      'Tu-who;
Tu-whit, tu-who' – a merry note,
While greasy Joan doth keel the pot.

When all aloud the wind doth blow,
   And coughing drowns the parson's saw,
And birds sit brooding in the snow,
   And Marian's nose looks red and raw,
When roasted crabs hiss in the bowl,
Then nightly sings the staring owl,
      'Tu-who;
Tu-whit, tu-who' – a merry note,
While greasy Joan doth keel the pot.

PERCY BYSSHE SHELLEY
1792–1822

───── ∞∞∞ ─────

Shelley was born on 9 August 1792 at Field Place, Warnham, near Horsham in Sussex. He was educated at Eton and University College, Oxford, but was sent down after writing an atheist pamphlet. Virtually disowned by his father, he and his equally radical friend Thomas Hogg took rooms at 15 Poland Street in Soho before Shelley eloped with Harriet Westbrook and married her in Edinburgh in August 1811. The relationship soon crumbled under the weight of Shelley's unconventional views on religion and the royal family, and his attempt to set up a *ménage à trois* with Hogg.

Shelley spent the next few years trying to establish communes in Devon and North Wales and fathering children on both his wife and his mistress. In the spring of 1818 he and his family took off for Italy, where both infants died. The birth of another son, however, seemed to restore Shelley's spirits and his poetic output increased. In April 1822, on Shelley's return from a visit to Byron and Leigh Hunt in Leghorn, the boat carrying him and his friend Edward Williams sank in a storm, although there were signs they were boarded, possibly by Italian pirates. Shelley's body was cremated on the beach and his ashes buried under the wine cellars in the house of the British Consul in Rome.

50

OZYMANDIAS OF EGYPT

I met a traveller from an antique land
Who said: Two vast and trunkless legs of stone
Stand in the desert . . . Near them, on the sand,
Half sunk, a shattered visage lies, whose frown,
And wrinkled lip, and sneer of cold command,
Tell that its sculptor well those passions read
Which yet survive, stamped on these lifeless things,
The hand that mocked them, and the heart that fed;
And on the pedestal these words appear:
'My name is Ozymandias, king of kings:
Look on my works, ye Mighty, and despair!'
Nothing beside remains. Round the decay
Of that colossal wreck, boundless and bare,
The lone and level sands stretch far away.

$\boxed{93}$

TO A SKYLARK

Hail to thee, blithe Spirit!
   Bird thou never wert,
That from Heaven, or near it,
   Pourest thy full heart
In profuse strains of unpremeditated art.

Higher still and higher
   From the earth thou springest
Like a cloud of fire;
   The blue deep thou wingest,
And singing still dost soar, and soaring ever singest.

In the golden lightning
   Of the sunken sun,
O'er which clouds are bright'ning,
   Thou dost float and run;
Like an unbodied joy whose race is just begun.

The pale purple even
   Melts around thy flight;
Like a star of Heaven,
   In the broad daylight
Thou art unseen, but yet I hear thy shrill delight.

Keen as are the arrows
  Of that silver sphere,
Whose intense lamp narrows
  In the white dawn clear
Until we hardly see – we feel that it is there.

All the earth and air
  With thy voice is loud,
As, when night is bare,
  From one lonely cloud
The moon rains out her beams, and Heaven is overflowed.

What thou art we know not;
  What is most like thee?
From rainbow clouds there flow not
  Drops so bright to see
As from thy presence showers a rain of melody.

Like a Poet hidden
  In the light of thought,
Singing hymns unbidden,
  Till the world is wrought
To sympathy with hopes and fears it heeded not:

Like a high-born maiden
  In a palace-tower,
Soothing her love-laden
  Soul in secret hour
With music sweet as love, which overflows her bower:

Like a glow-worm golden
   In a dell of dew,
Scattering unbeholden
   Its aëreal hue
Among the flowers and grass, which screen it from the
   view!

Like a rose embowered
   In its own green leaves,
By warm winds deflowered,
   Till the scent it gives
Makes faint with too much sweet those heavy-wingèd
   thieves:

Sound of vernal showers
   On the twinkling grass,
Rain-awakened flowers,
   All that ever was
Joyous, and clear, and fresh, thy music doth surpass:

Teach us, Sprite or Bird,
   What sweet thoughts are thine:
I have never heard
   Praise of love or wine
That panted forth a flood of rapture so divine.

Chorus Hymeneal,
   Or triumphal chant,
Matched with thine would be all
   But an empty vaunt,
A thing wherein we feel there is some hidden want.

Percy Bysshe Shelley

What objects are the fountains
  Of thy happy strain?
What fields, or waves, or mountains?
  What shapes of sky or plain?
What love of thine own kind? what ignorance of pain?

With thy clear keen joyance
  Languor cannot be:
Shadow of annoyance
  Never came near thee:
Thou lovest – but ne'er knew love's sad satiety.

Waking or asleep,
  Thou of death must deem
Things more true and deep
  Than we mortals dream,
Or how could thy notes flow in such a crystal stream?

We look before and after,
  And pine for what is not:
Our sincerest laughter
  With some pain is fraught;
Our sweetest songs are those that tell of saddest thought.

Yet if we could scorn
  Hate, and pride, and fear;
If we were things born
  Not to shed a tear,
I know not how thy joy we ever should come near.

Better than all measures
  Of delightful sound,
Better than all treasures
  That in books are found,
Thy skill to poet were, thou scorner of the ground!

Teach me half the gladness
  That thy brain must know,
Such harmonious madness
  From my lips would flow
The world should listen then – as I am listening now.

STEVIE SMITH
1902–71

—————— ✺ ——————

Florence Margaret Smith was born on 20 September 1902 in Hull and nicknamed Stevie after the ten times champion jockey Steve Donoghue. At the age of three, Stevie and her sister were taken by their mother to London to be cared for by Aunt Madge, 'The Lion Aunt', at her house in Palmers Green. After attending Palmers Green High School and the North London Collegiate School for Girls, Stevie worked as a secretary in publishing while her social life revolved around the local church. She began to write poetry and a novel, and one of her poems was read, at George Orwell's suggestion, by Sir Herbert Read on the BBC in 1942. During the 1950s and 1960s she enjoyed considerable success, making public appearances at poetry and jazz events. In 1977 Hugh Whitemore's play *Stevie*, later filmed with Glenda Jackson in the title role, was a great success in London and New York.

66

NOT WAVING BUT DROWNING

Nobody heard him, the dead man,
But still he lay moaning:
I was much further out than you thought
And not waving but drowning.

Poor chap, he always loved larking
And now he's dead
It must have been too cold for him his heart gave way,
They said.

Oh, no no no, it was too cold always
(Still the dead one lay moaning)
I was much too far out all my life
And not waving but drowning.

ALFRED, LORD TENNYSON
1809–92

———— ❦ ————

Tennyson was born on 6 August 1809 at Somersby, Lincolnshire, the third surviving son of the local rector, and
educated at Louth Grammar School and Trinity College,
Cambridge. There he was elected to the Society of Apostles,
won a Chancellor's Medal in 1829 and became a close
friend of Arthur Hallam, whose early death four years later
caused a grief-stricken Tennyson to write 'In Memoriam'.
He became engaged to Emily Sellwood but delayed the
marriage until 1850, possibly fearing that he had inherited
epilepsy and might pass it on to his children. In the same
year he was appointed Poet Laureate, much to the delight of
two of Tennyson's most devoted admirers, Prince Albert
and Queen Victoria. He named his son Hallam after his old
friend, and built a house near Haslemere in Surrey for his
family in 1868. It was there that he died on 6 October 1892.

5

THE LADY OF SHALOTT

I

On either side the river lie
Long fields of barley and of rye,
That clothe the wold and meet the sky;
And thro' the field the road runs by
  To many-tower'd Camelot;
And up and down the people go,
Gazing where the lilies blow
Round an island there below,
  The island of Shalott.

Willows whiten, aspens quiver,
Little breezes dusk and shiver
Thro' the wave that runs for ever
By the island in the river
  Flowing down to Camelot.
Four grey walls, and four grey towers,
Overlook a space of flowers,
And the silent isle imbowers
  The Lady of Shalott.

By the margin, willow-veil'd,
Slide the heavy barges trail'd
By slow horses; and unhail'd
The shallop flitteth silken-sail'd
   Skimming down to Camelot:
But who hath seen her wave her hand?
Or at the casement seen her stand?
Or is she known in all the land,
   The Lady of Shalott?

Only reapers, reaping early
In among the bearded barley,
Hear a song that echoes cheerly
From the river winding clearly,
   Down to tower'd Camelot:
And by the moon the reaper weary
Piling sheaves in uplands airy,
Listening, whispers, ''Tis the fairy
   Lady of Shalott.'

    II
There she weaves by night and day
A magic web with colours gay.
She has heard a whisper say,
A curse is on her if she stay
   To look down to Camelot.
She knows not what the curse may be,
And so she weaveth steadily,
And little other care hath she,
   The Lady of Shalott.

And moving through a mirror clear
That hangs before her all the year,
Shadows of the world appear.
There she sees the highway near
      Winding down to Camelot;
There the river eddy whirls,
And there the surly village churls,
And the red cloaks of market girls
      Pass onward from Shalott.

Sometimes a troop of damsels glad,
An abbot on an ambling pad,
Sometimes a curly shepherd lad,
Or long-hair'd page in crimson clad
      Goes by to tower'd Camelot;
And sometimes through the mirror blue
The knights come riding two and two.
She hath no loyal Knight and true,
      The Lady of Shalott.

But in her web she still delights
To weave the mirror's magic sights,
For often through the silent nights
A funeral, with plumes and lights
      And music, went to Camelot;
Or when the Moon was overhead,
Came two young lovers lately wed.
'I am half sick of shadows,' said
      The Lady of Shalott.

III

A bow-shot from her bower-eaves,
He rode between the barley sheaves,
The sun came dazzling thro' the leaves,
And flamed upon the brazen greaves
   Of bold Sir Lancelot.
A red-cross knight for ever kneel'd
To a lady in his shield,
That sparkled on the yellow field,
   Beside remote Shalott.

The gemmy bridle glitter'd free,
Like to some branch of stars we see
Hung in the golden Galaxy.
The bridle bells rang merrily
   As he rode down to Camelot:
And from his blazon'd baldric slung
A mighty silver bugle hung,
And as he rode his armor rung
   Beside remote Shalott.

All in the blue unclouded weather
Thick-jewell'd shone the saddle-leather,
The helmet and the helmet-feather
Burn'd like one burning flame together,
   As he rode down to Camelot.
As often thro' the purple night,
Below the starry clusters bright,
Some bearded meteor, burning bright,
   Moves over still Shalott.

His broad clear brow in sunlight glow'd;
On burnish'd hooves his war-horse trode;
From underneath his helmet flow'd
His coal-black curls as on he rode,
     As he rode down to Camelot.
From the bank and from the river
He flashed into the crystal mirror,
'Tirra lirra,' by the river
     Sang Sir Lancelot.

She left the web, she left the loom,
She made three paces through the room,
She saw the water-lily bloom,
She saw the helmet and the plume,
     She look'd down to Camelot.
Out flew the web and floated wide;
The mirror crack'd from side to side;
'The curse is come upon me,' cried
     The Lady of Shalott.

IV

In the stormy east-wind straining,
The pale yellow woods were waning,
The broad stream in his banks complaining.
Heavily the low sky raining
     Over tower'd Camelot;
Down she came and found a boat
Beneath a willow left afloat,
And around about the prow she wrote
     The Lady of Shalott.

And down the river's dim expanse
Like some bold seer in a trance,
Seeing all his own mischance –
With a glassy countenance
      Did she look to Camelot.
And at the closing of the day
She loosed the chain, and down she lay;
The broad stream bore her far away,
      The Lady of Shalott.

Lying, robed in snowy white
That loosely flew to left and right –
The leaves upon her falling light –
Thro' the noises of the night,
      She floated down to Camelot:
And as the boat-head wound along
The willowy hills and fields among,
They heard her singing her last song,
      The Lady of Shalott.

Heard a carol, mournful, holy,
Chanted loudly, chanted lowly,
Till her blood was frozen slowly,
And her eyes were darkened wholly,
      Turn'd to tower'd Camelot.
For ere she reach'd upon the tide
The first house by the water-side,
Singing in her song she died,
      The Lady of Shalott.

Under tower and balcony,
By garden-wall and gallery,
A gleaming shape she floated by,
Dead-pale between the houses high,
      Silent into Camelot.
Out upon the wharfs they came,
Knight and Burgher, Lord and Dame,
And around the prow they read her name,
      The Lady of Shalott.

Who is this? And what is here?
And in the lighted palace near
Died the sound of royal cheer;
And they crossed themselves for fear,
      All the Knights at Camelot;
But Lancelot mused a little space;
He said, 'She has a lovely face;
God in his mercy lend her grace,
      The Lady of Shalott.'

58

THE CHARGE OF THE LIGHT BRIGADE

I

Half a league, half a league,
    Half a league onward,
All in the valley of Death
    Rode the six hundred.
'Forward, the Light Brigade!
Charge for the guns!' he said;
Into the valley of Death
    Rode the six hundred.

II

'Forward, the Light Brigade!'
Was there a man dismay'd?
Not tho' the soldier knew
    Some one had blunder'd:
Their's not to make reply,
Their's not to reason why,
Their's but to do and die:
Into the valley of Death
    Rode the six hundred.

III

Cannon to right of them,
Cannon to left of them,
Cannon in front of them
  Volley'd and thunder'd;
Storm'd at with shot and shell,
Boldly they rode and well,
Into the jaws of Death,
Into the mouth of Hell
  Rode the six hundred.

IV

Flash'd all their sabres bare,
Flash'd as they turn'd in air,
Sabring the gunners there,
Charging an army, while
  All the world wonder'd:
Plunged in the battery-smoke
Right thro' the line they broke;
Cossack and Russian
Reel'd from the sabre-stroke
  Shatter'd and sunder'd.
Then they rode back, but not,
  Not the six hundred.

V

Cannon to right of them,
Cannon to left of them,
Cannon behind them
 Volley'd and thunder'd;
Storm'd at with shot and shell,
While horse and hero fell,
They that had fought so well
Came thro' the jaws of Death
Back from the mouth of Hell,
All that was left of them,
 Left of six hundred.

VI

When can their glory fade?
O the wild charge they made!
 All the world wonder'd.
Honour the charge they made!
Honour the Light Brigade,
 Noble six hundred!

71

CROSSING THE BAR

Sunset and evening star,
  And one clear call for me!
And may there be no moaning of the bar,
  When I put out to sea,

But such a tide as moving seems asleep,
  Too full for sound and foam,
When that which drew from out the boundless deep
  Turns again home.

Twilight and evening bell,
  And after that the dark!
And may there be no sadness of farewell,
  When I embark;

For tho' from out our bourne of Time and Place
  The flood may bear me far,
I hope to see my Pilot face to face
  When I have crosst the bar.

DYLAN THOMAS
1914–53

———— ❊ ————

Dylan Marlais Thomas was born on 27 October 1914 in Swansea, the son of the senior English master at the local grammar school where Thomas himself was educated. After school he worked for three years as a reporter on the *South Wales Evening Post* before moving to London in 1934. Thanks to the influence of Edith Sitwell, his first collection of verse was published shortly after his arrival in the capital. In 1937 he married Caitlin Macnamara, who was to bear him three children. He was a heavy drinker and smoker, a hell-raiser and womaniser, and it could be argued that his bad habits impaired his poetic gifts; but certainly his poor health excused him from military service and he spent the war as a freelance broadcaster and working in a film documentary unit. He returned with his family to Wales in 1949 and, although his poetic output diminished in the 1950s, he did write what is probably his best-known work – the radio play *Under Milk Wood.* In 1950 he began a series of lecture tours of the United States and it was in New York, on 9 November 1953, that he collapsed from alcoholic poisoning and died at the age of thirty-nine. His 'Do Not Go Gentle into That Good Night' encapsulates something about Thomas's fear of, and fascination with, death. It was inspired by his father's impending blindness.

37

DO NOT GO GENTLE
INTO THAT GOOD NIGHT

Do not go gentle into that good night,
Old age should burn and rave at close of day;
Rage, rage against the dying of the light.

Though wise men at their end know dark is right,
Because their words had forked no lightning they
Do not go gentle into that good night.

Good men, the last wave by, crying how bright
Their frail deeds might have danced in a green bay,
Rage, rage against the dying of the light.

Wild men who caught and sang the sun in flight,
And learn, too late, they grieved it on its way,
Do not go gentle into that good night.

Grave men, near death, who see with blinding sight
Blind eyes could blaze like meteors and be gay,
Rage, rage against the dying of the light.

And you, my father, there on the sad height,
Curse, bless, me now with your fierce tears, I pray.
Do not go gentle into that good night.
Rage, rage against the dying of the light.

$\boxed{56}$

FERN HILL

Now as I was young and easy under the apple boughs
About the lilting house and happy as the grass was green,
   The night above the dingle starry,
     Time let me hail and climb
    Golden in the heydays of his eyes,
And honoured among wagons I was prince of the apple
   towns
And once below a time I lordly had the trees and leaves
    Trail with daisies and barley
   Down the rivers of the windfall light.

And as I was green and carefree, famous among the barns
About the happy yard and singing as the farm was home,
   In the sun that is young once only,
     Time let me play and be
    Golden in the mercy of his means,
And green and golden I was huntsman and herdsman, the
   calves
Sang to my horn, the foxes on the hills barked clear and
   cold,
    And the sabbath rang slowly
   In the pebbles of the holy streams.

All the sun long it was running, it was lovely, the hay
Fields high as the house, the tunes from the chimneys, it
  was air
   And playing, lovely and watery
     And fire green as grass.
   And nightly under the simple stars
As I rode to sleep the owls were bearing the farm away,
All the moon long I heard, blessed among stables, the
  nightjars
   Flying with the ricks, and the horses
     Flashing into the dark.

And then to awake, and the farm, like a wanderer white
With the dew, come back, the cock on his shoulder: it was
  all
   Shining, it was Adam and maiden,
     The sky gathered again
   And the sun grew round that very day.
So it must have been after the birth of the simple light
In the first, spinning place, the spellbound horses walking
  warm
   Out of the whinnying green stable
     On to the fields of praise.

And honoured among foxes and pheasants by the gay
  house
Under the new made clouds and happy as the heart was
  long,

In the sun born over and over,
   I ran my heedless ways,
My wishes raced through the house high hay
And nothing I cared, at my sky blue trades, that time allows
In all his tuneful turning so few and such morning songs
   Before the children green and golden
     Follow him out of grace.

Nothing I cared, in the lamb white days, that time would
   take me
Up to the swallow thronged loft by the shadow of my hand,
   In the moon that is always rising,
     Nor that riding to sleep
   I should hear him fly with the high fields
And wake to the farm forever fled from the childless land.
Oh as I was young and easy in the mercy of his means,
   Time held me green and dying
  Though I sang in my chains like the sea.

EDWARD THOMAS
1878–1917

———❦———

Philip Edward Thomas was born on 3 March 1878, in London, the first of six sons born to a Welsh couple. After his education at Battersea Grammar School and St Paul's, he worked for a year as a clerk in the Board of Trade before taking up a scholarship to read history at London University. He married in 1899 without the knowledge of his parents and became a father a year later. Thomas decided to support himself and his growing family through his writing, a decision which was to cause constant worry and financial hardship. He continued on the literary treadmill until he met Robert Frost and through him became part of the circle of Dymock Poets. Thomas was killed on active service during the First World War at Arras on 9 April 1917.

23

ADLESTROP

Yes. I remember Adlestrop –
The name, because one afternoon
Of heat the express-train drew up there
Unwontedly. It was late June.

The steam hissed. Someone cleared his throat.
No one left and no one came
On the bare platform. What I saw
Was Adlestrop – only the name

And willows, willow-herb, and grass,
And meadowsweet, and haycocks dry,
No whit less still and lonely fair
Than the high cloudlets in the sky.

And for that minute a blackbird sang
Close by, and around him, mistier,
Farther and farther, all the birds
Of Oxfordshire and Gloucestershire.

FRANCIS THOMPSON
1859–1907

Francis Thompson was born on 18 December 1859, the son of a staunchly Catholic doctor, in Preston, Lancashire, and educated at Ushaw College. His early intention of becoming a priest came to nothing, and he failed to qualify to follow his father into the medical profession. In 1885 he left for London where he took a series of dead-end jobs to finance his growing opium habit. He was rescued from this degradation by the writers Wilfrid and Alice Meynell. They introduced him to the poet Coventry Patmore, who placed him in the care of monks at Storrington in Sussex and then in Wales. His continued addiction and an attack of tuberculosis led to his early death on 13 November 1907. His tomb is inscribed with a line from his poem 'The Hound of Heaven': 'Look for me in the nurseries of Heaven'.

83

From THE HOUND OF HEAVEN

I fled Him, down the nights and down the days;
  I fled Him down the arches of the years;
I fled Him. Down the labyrinthine ways
  Of my own mind; and in the mist of tears
I hid from Him, and under running laughter.
      Up vistaed hopes I sped;
      And shot, precipitated.
Adown Titanic glooms of chasmèd fears,
  From those strong Feet that followed, followed after.
    But with unhurrying chase,
    And unperturbed pace,
Deliberate speed, majestic instancy
    They beat – and a Voice beat
    More instant than the Feet –
'All things betray thee, who betrayest Me.'

  I pleaded, outlaw-wise,
By many a hearted casement, curtained red,
  Trellised with intertwining charities;
(For, though I knew His love Who followèd,
  Yet was I sore adread
Lest, having Him, I must have naught beside);
But, if one little casement parted wide,
  The gust of His approach would clash it to.
Fear wist not to evade, as Love wist to pursue.

Across the margent of the world I fled,
   And troubled the gold gateways of the stars,
   Smiting for shelter on their clangèd bars;
      Fretted to dulcet jars
And silvern chatter the pale ports o' the moon.
I said to dawn, Be sudden; to eve, Be soon;
   With thy young skiey blossoms heap me over
         From this tremendous Lover!
Float thy vague veil about me, lest He see!
   I tempted all His servitors, but to find
My own betrayal in their constancy,
In faith to Him their fickleness to me,
   Their traitorous trueness, and their loyal deceit.
To all swift things for swiftness did I sue;
Clung to the whistling mane of every wind.
   But whether they swept, smoothly fleet,
   The long savannahs of the blue;
         Or whether, Thunder-driven,
   They clanged his chariot 'thwart a heaven
Plashy with flying lightnings round the spurn o' their feet:
   Fear wist not to evade as Love wist to pursue.

         Still with unhurrying chase,
         And unperturbèd pace,
Deliberate speed, majestic instancy,
         Came on the following Feet,
         And a Voice above their beat –
'Naught shelters thee who wilt not shelter Me.'

* * *

265

Now of that long pursuit
Comes on at hand the bruit:
That Voice is round me like a bursting sea:
'And is thy earth so marred,
Shattered in shard on shard?
Lo, all things fly thee, for thou fliest Me!
Strange, piteous, futile thing,
Wherefore should any set thee love apart?
Seeing none but I makes much of naught' (He said)
'And human love needs human meriting:
How hast thou merited –
Of all man's clotted clay the dingiest clot?
Alack, thou knowest not
How little worthy of any love thou art!
Whom wilt thou find to love ignoble thee
Save Me, save only Me?
All which I took from thee I did but take,
Not for thy harms,
But just that thou might'st seek it in My arms.
All which thy child's mistake
Fancies as lost, I have stored for thee at home:
Rise, clasp My hand, and come!'

Halts by me that footfall:
Is my gloom, after all,
Shade of His hand, outstretched caressingly?
'Ah, fondest, blindest, weakest,
I am He Whom thou seekest!
Thou dravest love from thee, who dravest Me.'

OSCAR WILDE
1854–1900

Oscar Fingal O'Flahertie Wills Wilde was born on 16 October 1854 in Dublin, the son of an eminent eye surgeon and an artistically inclined mother. After graduating from Trinity College, Dublin, he went to Magdalen College, Oxford, where he remained from 1874 to 1879, moving to London in the early 1880s. He had already had work published in Irish magazines and periodicals, and continued to produce large numbers of stories and poems. After marrying Constance Lloyd in 1884 he fathered two sons: Cyril, born in 1885, and Vyvyan, born in 1886.

His success as a playwright in the 1890s, with such works as *An Ideal Husband* and *The Importance of Being Earnest*, was brought to an abrupt end when he was accused by the Marquess of Queensberry, the choleric father of his young intimate, Lord Alfred Douglas (Bosie), of posing as a 'somdomite' (*sic*). The case led to a trial which exposed Wilde's homosexual lifestyle, then illegal, and he was sentenced to two years' imprisonment in Reading Gaol from where he wrote 'De Profundis', his famous letter to Bosie. He was released from prison, a broken man, and fled to France where he died in poverty on 30 November 1900. 'The Ballad of Reading Gaol' was originally published under Wilde's prison number, C3.3.

45

From THE BALLAD OF READING GAOL

He did not wear his scarlet coat,
    For blood and wine are red,
And blood and wine were on his hands
    When they found him with the dead,
The poor dead woman whom he loved,
    And murdered in her bed.

He walked amongst the Trial Men
    In a suit of shabby grey;
A cricket cap was on his head,
    And his step seemed light and gay;
But I never saw a man who looked
    So wistfully at the day.

I never saw a man who looked
    With such a wistful eye
Upon that little tent of blue
    Which prisoners call the sky,
And at every drifting cloud that went
    With sails of silver by.

I walked, with other souls in pain,
    Within another ring,
And was wondering if the man had done
    A great or little thing,
When a voice behind me whispered low,
    That fellow's got to swing!

* * *

Six weeks our guardsman walked the yard,
    In the suit of shabby grey:
His cricket cap was on his head,
    And his step seemed light and gay,
But I never saw a man who looked
    So wistfully at the day.

I never saw a man who looked
    With such a wistful eye
Upon that little tent of blue
    Which prisoners call the sky,
And at every wandering cloud that trailed
    Its ravelled fleeces by.

He did not wring his hands, as do
    Those witless men who dare
To try to rear the changeling Hope
    In the cave of black Despair:
He only looked upon the sun,
    And drank the morning air.

He did not wring his hands nor weep,
    Nor did he peek or pine,
But he drank the air as though it held
    Some healthful anodyne;
With open mouth he drank the sun
    As though it had been wine!

And I and all the souls in pain,
    Who tramped the other ring,
Forgot if we ourselves had done
    A great or little thing,
And watched with gaze of dull amaze
    The man who had to swing.

And strange it was to see him pass
    With a step so light and gay,
And strange it was to see him look
    So wistfully at the day,
And strange it was to think that he
    Had such a debt to pay.

WILLIAM WORDSWORTH
1770–1850

———∞∞∞———

Wordsworth was born on 7 April 1770 in Cockermouth, Cumberland, the son of a solicitor and law agent, and educated at Hawkshead School and St John's College, Cambridge. He began to write poetry as a young man and was also an enthusiastic walker, tramping through Wales, across Salisbury Plain and France, where he found himself just as the Revolution was sweeping away the monarchy. An affair in France with a woman named Annette Vallon produced a daughter, but in 1802 he married Mary Hutchinson. He joined his fellow poets Coleridge and Southey, migrating to the same area of Somerset but they were forced to leave by the locals, suspicious of their eccentric lifestyle. Wordsworth and his sister Dorothy eventually returned to their beloved Lake District, living for more than thirty years at Rydal Mount in Grasmere.

Tennyson considered Wordsworth to be the greatest poet ever, and on the death of Southey in 1843 Wordsworth reluctantly succeeded his friend in the post of Poet Laureate. He died on 23 April 1850 at the age of eighty.

1

THE DAFFODILS

I wander'd lonely as a cloud
That floats on high o'er vales and hills,
When all at once I saw a crowd,
A host of golden daffodils,
Beside the lake, beneath the trees
Fluttering and dancing in the breeze.

Continuous as the stars that shine
And twinkle on the milky way,
They stretch'd in never-ending line
Along the margin of a bay:
Ten thousand saw I at a glance
Tossing their heads in sprightly dance.

The waves beside them danced, but they
Out-did the sparkling waves in glee: –
A Poet could not but be gay
In such a jocund company!
I gazed – and gazed – but little thought
What wealth the show to me had brought.

For oft, when on my couch I lie
In vacant or in pensive mood,
They flash upon that inward eye
Which is the bliss of solitude;
And then my heart with pleasure fills,
And dances with the daffodils.

15

UPON WESTMINSTER BRIDGE

Sept. 3, 1802

Earth has not anything to show more fair:
Dull would he be of soul who could pass by
A sight so touching in its majesty:
This City now doth like a garment wear

The beauty of the morning: silent, bare,
Ships, towers, domes, theatres, and temples lie
Open unto the fields, and to the sky,
All bright and glittering in the smokeless air.

Never did sun more beautifully steep
In his first splendour valley, rock, or hill;
Ne'er saw I, never felt, a calm so deep!

The river glideth at his own sweet will:
Dear God! the very houses seem asleep;
And all that mighty heart is lying still!

96

THE SOLITARY REAPER

Behold her, single in the field,
Yon solitary Highland Lass!
Reaping and singing by herself;
Stop here, or gently pass!
Alone she cuts and binds the grain,
And sings a melancholy strain;
O listen! for the Vale profound
Is overflowing with the sound.

No Nightingale did ever chaunt
So sweetly to reposing bands
Of Travellers in some shady haunt,
Among Arabian Sands:
No sweeter voice was ever heard
In spring-time from the Cuckoo-bird,
Breaking the silence of the seas
Among the farthest Hebrides.

Will no one tell me what she sings? –
Perhaps the plaintive numbers flow
For old, unhappy, far-off things,
And battles long ago:
Or is it some more humble lay,
Familiar matter of today?
Some natural sorrow, loss or pain,
That has been, and may be again!

Whate'er the theme, the Maiden sang
As if her song could have no ending;
I saw her singing at her work,
And o'er the sickle bending;
I listened till I had my fill:
And, as I mounted up the hill,
The music in my heart I bore,
Long after it was heard no more.

W. B. YEATS
1865–1939

William Butler Yeats was born on 3 June 1865 in Sandy-mount, County Dublin, the eldest son of a painter. Fascinated from an early age by mysticism and the supernatural, Yeats was equally captivated by Irish folklore and was a fervent Nationalist. He helped to found the Irish Literary Society in London in 1891 and in Dublin the following year. In 1904 the Irish National Theatre began life at the Abbey Theatre in Dublin, set up partly as a result of Yeats' commitment and energy. His Nationalist zeal was fired by his unrequited passion for Maud Gonne, and he seemed to lose a little of his belief in the cause after her marriage in 1903.

For all his Irish patriotism Yeats lived for long periods of his life in London. As a boy he attended school in Hammersmith and lived in a house in Primrose Hill where the American poet Sylvia Plath was later to be based. He spent twenty-four years in Bloomsbury where he befriended the American poet Ezra Pound who was to be Yeats' best man at his wedding in 1917. After Ireland won independence, Yeats served as a Senator of the Irish Free State from 1923 to 1928. He won the Nobel Prize in 1923 and died at Cap Martin in France on 28 January 1939. Yeats said he wrote 'The Lake Isle of Innisfree' when reminded of the holidays of his childhood by a novelty fountain in the window of a shop in Fleet Street.

17

THE LAKE ISLE OF INNISFREE

I will arise and go now, and go to Innisfree,
And a small cabin build there, of clay and wattles made:
Nine bean-rows will I have there, a hive for the honey-bee,
And live alone in the bee-loud glade.

And I shall have some peace there, for peace comes
    dropping slow,
Dropping from the veils of the morning to where the
    cricket sings;
There midnight's all a glimmer, and noon a purple glow,
    And evening full of the linnet's wings.

I will arise and go now, for always night and day
I hear lake water lapping with low sounds by the shore;
While I stand on the roadway, or on the pavements grey,
I hear it in the deep heart's core.

21

HE WISHES FOR THE CLOTHS OF HEAVEN

Had I the heavens' embroidered cloths,
Enwrought with golden and silver light,
The blue and the dim and the dark cloths
Of night and light and the half-light,
I would spread the cloths under your feet:
But I, being poor, have only my dreams;
I have spread my dreams under your feet;
Tread softly because you tread on my dreams.

46

WHEN YOU ARE OLD

When you are old and grey and full of sleep,
And nodding by the fire, take down this book,
And slowly read, and dream of the soft look
Your eyes had once, and of their shadows deep;

How many loved your moments of glad grace,
And loved your beauty with love false or true,
But one man loved the pilgrim soul in you,
And loved the sorrows of your changing face;

And bending down beside the glowing bars,
Murmur, a little sadly, how Love fled
And paced upon the mountains overhead
And hid his face amid a crowd of stars.

Acknowledgements

The publishers would like to acknowledge the following for permission to reproduce copyright material:

A. P. Watt Ltd on behalf of The National Trust for Places of Historic Interest or Natural Beauty for *'If'*, *'The Way Through the Woods'* and *'The Glory of the Garden'* from *Rudyard Kipling's Verse: Definitive Edition*.

The Literary Trustees of Walter de la Mare and the Society of Authors as their representatives for *'The Listeners'* and *'Silver'*.

The Society of Authors as the literary representative of the Estate of John Masefield for *'Cargoes'*, *'Sea Fever'* and *'Reynard The Fox'*.

'Leisure' from the *Complete Poems of W. H. Davies* published by Jonathan Cape.

The Society of Authors as the literary representative of the Estate of A. E. Housman for *'Loveliest of Trees, the Cherry Now'*.

John Murray (Publishers) Ltd for *'The Highwayman'* by Alfred Noyes from his *Collected Poems*.

A. P. Watt on behalf of Michael Yeats for *'The Lake Isle of Innisfree'*, *'He Wishes for the Cloths of Heaven'* and *'When You Are Old'* from *The Collected Poems of W. B. Yeats*.

John Murray (Publishers) Ltd for *'Christmas'*, *'Diary of a Church Mouse'*, *'A Subaltern's Love-Song'*, *'Hunter Trials'*, *'Myfanwy'* and *'Slough'* by John Betjeman from his *Collected Poems*.

This England magazine for permission to reproduce *'High Flight'* by John Gillespie Magee.

Faber and Faber Ltd for *'Journey of the Magi'*, *'Macavity the Mystery Cat'* and *'The Waste Land'* by T. S. Eliot.

'Stopping by Woods on a Snowy Evening' and *'The Road Not Taken'* from *The*

Acknowledgements

Poetry of Robert Frost edited by Edward Connery Lathem, published by Jonathan Cape.

A. P. Watt on behalf of the literary estate of G. K. Chesterton for *'The Donkey'* and *'Lepanto'*.

David Higham Associates on behalf of the literary estate of Dylan Thomas for *'Do Not Go Gentle into That Good Night'* and *'Fern Hill'* from *The Poems*/Dylan Thomas.

Faber and Faber Ltd for *'Stop All the Clocks'* and *'Night Mail'* by W. H. Auden from his *Collected Poems*.

John Johnson for *'Warning'* from *Selected Poems* by Jenny Joseph.

'Everyone Sang' by Siegfried Sassoon, reprinted by permission of George Sassoon.

'Vitae Lampada' and *'He Fell Among Thieves'* by Sir Henry Newbolt, reprinted by permission of Peter Newbolt.

Faber and Faber Ltd for *'The Whitsun Weddings'* from *Collected Poems* by Philip Larkin.

James MacGibbon for *'Not Waving but Drowning'* from *The Collected Poems of Stevie Smith* (Penguin Twentieth Century Classics).

Papermac for *'Weathers'* from *The Complete Poems of Thomas Hardy*.

Laurence Pollinger Ltd and the Estate of Frieda Lawrence Ravagli for *'Snake'* from *The Complete Poems of D. H. Lawrence*.

Pan Macmillan for *'The Ice-Cart'* by Wilfrid Gibson.

Peters Fraser and Dunlop Group for *'Tarantella'* by Hilaire Belloc.

Pan Macmillan for *'The Bells of Heaven'* by Ralph Hodgson.

In addition the publishers would like to thank Al Senter who collated the text, Anne Harvey for her technical advice, and all at Heavy Entertainment.

INDEX OF POEMS BY TITLE

Index of Poems by Title

INDEX OF FIRST LINES

Index of First Lines